THE
BONAPARTES

A tapestry showing the arms of the Napoleonic Empire, including the golden bees adopted by Napoleon: by Dubois.

FELIX MARKHAM

THE
BONAPARTES

Taplinger Publishing Company
New York

First published in the United States in 1975 by
Taplinger Publishing Co., Inc.
New York, New York

Library of Congress Catalog Card Number: 75-3637
ISBN 0-8008-0874-6

Contents

1 Corsican Origins

An extraordinary combination of circumstances was needed to promote the rise of the Bonapartes.

When J. J. Rousseau wrote of Corsica in 1762 in his *Contrat Social* that 'I have a presentiment that one day this small island will astonish Europe', he little guessed how his prediction would turn out.

Rousseau was thinking of a proud, small country fighting for independence against the domination of the Genoese. By 1761 the Corsican patriot Pasquale Paoli had unified the people, given them a constitution and repelled the Genoese. In 1766 James Boswell visited Corsica, and his *Account of Corsica* gave wide publicity to Paoli and the Corsican cause. Both the mountainous scenery and the clan society naturally reminded Boswell of the Scottish Highlanders. Society was based on the solidarity of the family, and disputes were settled by the private feuds of the vendetta.

The manners of the Corsicans have a great similarity with those of the ancient Germans, as described by Tacitus. They have not however the same habit of drinking: for they are extremely temperate. Their morals are strict and chaste to an uncommon degree, owing in part to good principles untouched by luxury; and partly to the exercise of private revenge against such as violate the honour of their women.

Boswell explains that Paoli tried to put down the custom of collateral vendetta: 'If a man had received an injury, and could not find a proper opportunity to be revenged on his enemy personally, he revenged himself on one of his relations. So barbarous a practice was the source of innumerable assassinations.' This tradition of collateral vendetta undoubtedly played a part in Napoleon's thinking which led to the execution of the Bourbon Duc d'Enghien in 1804. Reminiscing at St Helena, Napoleon remarked, 'A Corsican would never think of abandoning his cousin.' The importance of Napoleon's Corsican origin has often been exaggerated (as will later appear) but one of the enduring effects was his sense of family obligation, which was often to prevail against his political judgment. Hence it is possible to speak not only of the rise of Bonaparte but of the rise of the Bonapartes.

Napoleon's father, Carlo Buona Parte, was not only head of one of the leading families of Corsica but one of Paoli's lieutenants in the resistance to the Genoese. Paoli's success was short-lived. By a cynical bargain, France acquired by treaty the Genoese rights on Corsica, and in 1768 invaded in force. Paoli was defeated at the battle of Ponte Nuovo and forced into exile – in England, where he was hospitably received by Boswell and Samuel Johnson. Of Paoli, Boswell wrote, 'He just lives in the times of antiquity. He said to me "A young man who would form his mind to glory must not read modern memoirs, but Plutarch and Titus Livius." Having known so exalted a character, my sentiments of human nature were raised . . . and I was for the rest of my life set free from a slavish timidity in the presence of great men, for where shall I find a man greater than Paoli?'

Carlo Buona Parte had to make a crucial decision – to stay in Corsica, or to join Paoli in exile. He stayed, and made his peace with the French. Three months later his second son, Napoleone, was born in Ajaccio. He was given this name after an uncle who had recently died fighting the French, and it was originally that of an Egyptian martyr. If the decision had gone the other way, Napoleon would probably have started his career as a British army or navy officer. It is an intriguing speculation.

Having made his peace with the French, Carlo Buona Parte was admitted as a member of the French *noblesse*. In later years, Napoleon was irritated by references to his Corsican origin and his ancestry. At the time of his marriage to the Austrian Archduchess Marie-Louise, the Austrian genealogists industriously traced his ancestors to the rulers of Treviso. Napoleon impatiently replied, 'Permit me to be the Rudolph of my dynasty. He was referring to Rudolph of Habsburg, the progenitor of the Austrian dynasty. He regarded himself as a self-made man, by right of his sword and conquest. When later accused of favouring the *noblesse* of the *ancien régime*, he retorted 'Am I, after all, a noble, I, a poor Corsican squire?' This is a fairly accurate description. The French *noblesse* of the *ancien régime* included a great deal more than the English peerage, and they ranged from the great Court nobles such as the Rohans to the poor provincial squire, pushing his own plough. The majority of them had recently risen from the ranks of the bourgeoisie. The one essential qualification was to 'live nobly', abstaining from retail trade and manual occupations.

Napoleon's ancestry is, however, of considerable importance and interest, if only because it secured him his education and training as a professional artillery officer, and gave his family a leading role in Corsican politics, in his early years. By the loose standards of the French *noblesse*, his family were 'of ancient race' on both sides. The Buona Partes were a well-known medieval family of Florentine *condottieri*, a branch of whom had invaded and settled in Corsica in the late fifteenth century. His mother, Letizia Ramolino, was of equally ancient family, but stemming from Lombardy and related to the noble family of Coll' Alto. Her father held the important position under the Genoese of Inspector-General of Roads and Bridges, and she brought to the marriage a considerable dowry in land, worth about £7,000. Carlo inherited

Carlo Buona Parte with Letizia, on horseback in Corsica: an engraving from a contemporary biography. Soldiers are seen in the background.

OVERLEAF The country home of the Bonapartes at Ajaccio: a contemporary painting. Napoleon himself was born in the town.

a town- and a country-house, and several parcels of land. In a poor and frugal society, the young couple were the aristocratic leaders of society and politics in Ajaccio. The uncle, Archdeacon Lucciano, boasted that 'Never have the Bonapartes bought oil, wine or bread.'

Boswell says of Ajaccio that 'It is the prettiest town in Corsica. It has many handsome streets and beautiful walks, a citadel and palace of the Genoese governor. The inhabitants of this town are the genteelest people in the island, having had a good deal of intercourse with the French.' At St Helena Napoleon admitted that 'In the island we thought ourselves as good as the Bourbons; we really were.'

Admission of the Corsican nobility to the French *noblesse* had been recommended to Louis xvi by Monsieur de Marbeuf, the new French governor, an elderly, benevolent, conciliatory man. Boswell had met him:

I found M de Marbeuf a worthy, open-hearted Frenchman. It is a common and very great remark that one of the most agreeable characters in the world is a Frenchman who has served long in the army and has arrived at the age when the fire of youth is properly tempered. Such a character is gay without levity and judicious without severity. Such a character was the Count de Marbeuf, of an ancient family in Brittany, where there is more plainness of character than among the other French. He had been *gentilhomme de la chambre* to the worthy King Stanislas.

It was a natural step for him to befriend the Bonapartes, despite their connection with Paoli. Carlo was one of the leading citizens of Corsica, one of the few who knew the French language, trained in the law, with a university education and doctorate at Pisa. In 1774 Carlo made his first visit to Paris as one of the Corsican delegates appointed to congratulate Louis xvi on his accession. He was a handsome, attractive, plausible young man, extrovert and extravagant, with a strikingly beautiful young wife. Later on, there were malicious rumours that Marbeuf was more interested in the wife, and that Napoleon was his son. This was a possibility that Napoleon actually discussed with the mathematician Monge on their voyage to Egypt in 1798, but dismissed. It is difficult to see how the idea could be entertained, as all the Bonaparte children had strongly marked and similar features. Apart from the fact that Letizia was at Corte in the centre of the island when Napoleon was conceived, and Marbeuf was at the other end of the island,

OPPOSITE Carlo Buona Parte, father of the dynasty: a portrait by Girodet-Trioson. Though this charming fop managed to secure a good education for his offspring at public expense, their daily upbringing was entirely in the hands of the formidable Letizia.

Letizia's character and whole career made nonsense of the rumour. Corsican manners were very different from the loose morals of eighteenth-century France.

'Beautiful as one of the mythical Greek loves' was Napoleon's description of his mother. As a small girl, Letizia was known as 'Ajaccio's little wonder', with her black eyes, chestnut curls and classical features. She was no mere beauty, but endowed with a character of Roman strength and simplicity. Married at the age of fourteen to a man she loved, she never looked at another man, and all her energies were concentrated on her family and household. After her strenuous roamings in the *maquis* in 1768–9, she returned to the Casa Buonaparte in Ajaccio, a three-storeyed house, of which the first floor was occupied by Carlo's uncle, the Archdeacon Lucciano, who replaced Carlo's father as the family adviser, and the top floor by a cousin. It was, however, apparent that without Letizia's careful management of money (which later became her notorious parsimony), Carlo would have run the family on to the rocks with debt. Retaining a simple purity, she went daily to Mass: but she was never prim, puritanical or fanatical. In accordance with Corsican tradition, she was obedient and indulgent to her husband even in his extravagance. Boswell says, 'The Corsicans, like the Germans, are extremely indolent. The women do the greatest part of the drudgery work as is also the custom among the Scots Highlanders.' In the twenty years of her married life, she bore thirteen children, of whom eight survived infancy – Joseph, Napoleon, Lucien, Elisa, Louis, Pauline, Caroline and Jérôme. In Corsica their names were Italian – Giuseppe, Napoleone, Lucciano, Maria-Anna, Luigi, Maria-Paola, Maria-Annunziata and Girolamo. Carlo would have spoiled the children. It was left to Letizia to apply judicious firmness and discipline as well as a fierce maternal love. At St Helena Napoleon confessed, 'I was very well brought up by my mother. I owe her a great deal. She instilled into me pride and taught me good sense.' Even when he was seventeen, she gave him a good whipping for mimicking the rheumatic walk of his grandmother.

She was in advance of her age in insisting on daily baths, and the children had plenty of freedom to run wild in the fresh air. She set aside a large room where they could make as much noise as they liked. Letizia was not fussy, and believed in hard knocks as a part of life. Such was the character of the young wife and mother of Ajaccio; and such it remained throughout the eighty-

OPPOSITE Napoleon in his childhood, with the mother he adored, but perhaps also feared: a contemporary artist's impression.

six years of her life. Neither prosperity nor adversity had the power to dominate or alter it. 'Provided it lasts' was her comment on the headlong rise of the family. In the fragmentary memoirs she dictated at the end of her life, she makes a touching revelation: 'Every one called me the happiest mother in the world, yet my life has been a succession of sorrows and torments. Each time letters came, I feared to read the disastrous news of the Emperor's death on the battle field.' Stendhal considered that 'Few lives have been so free from hypocrisy and to my mind so noble as that of Mme Letizia Bonaparte.'

With a growing family, Carlo busied himself in finding the best and cheapest education for the elder sons. It seemed obvious that Joseph, the gentle character, should prepare for a career in the Church. Napoleon, a hardy, aggressive and fearless small boy, seemed already destined for the army or navy. Here the interest and influence of Marbeuf was decisive. His nephew was Bishop of Autun and was willing to nominate Joseph and Napoleon to places at the church-school at Autun. Marbeuf, in accordance with his policy, had recommended that the sons of the poor Corsican *noblesse* should be admitted to the French royal military academies, which were confined to the *noblesse*, but included free places as well as fee-paying pupils. The Minister of War, St Germain, had in 1776 reorganized and improved the royal schools, founding twelve in the provinces. It was essential for Carlo to visit Paris to verify with the herald's office the proofs of *noblesse* which would make Napoleon eligible for a free place. In December 1778 he took Joseph and Napoleon with him to France and left them both at the college at Autun. Napoleon spent only three months there and had a painful parting from his close companion and brother, for early in 1779 the Ministry of War notified Carlo that Napoleon had gained a free place at Brienne, in the region of Champagne. It was one of the better royal schools, and the Franciscans, who had originally run it as a private school, continued in charge. Work and discipline were hard, and for Napoleon even his annual holiday had to be spent at school. He was not to see Corsica again for eight years, when he was already a young man. In 1782 he was visited at Brienne by both his parents, and the impression of Letizia's beauty was not forgotten by Napoleon's fellow pupils.

Setting aside the legends which surround the school-days of a great man, we find, strangely enough, that the authentic picture of

Napoleon as a boy at Brienne was given by an English fellow-pupil, who published his recollections in 1797. Naturally enough, he was at first exposed to teasing and ragging because of his bad French and Corsican accent. His odd Christian name of Napoleone gave him the nickname of *'Paille-au-Nez'* ('straw-nose'). He was soon able to hold his own by violent retaliation and was left alone. He was at first solitary, morose and bookish, retiring to his private patch of garden. Later he acquired a few friends, and even became something of a leader. In the cold winter of 1783 he devised elaborate snow-forts in which he organized battles and sieges.

The annual reports of the Inspector of Royal Schools trace clearly Napoleon's scholastic progress. He was outstanding in mathematics, good in history, poor in languages. His mathematical excellence made him evidently suitable for the Navy, and the success of the French Navy in the American War of Independence fired Napoleon's ambition. In any case, the next step in his education would be entrance to the École Militaire in Paris, and the question of his career remained open when in 1784 the Inspector nominated him to the École. Before he left for Paris he was able to welcome his younger brother Lucien, who was succeeding to his free place at Brienne, and his father, who was also bringing his young sister Maria-Anna (Elisa) to a free place at the grand girls' school of St Cyr founded by Madame de Maintenon. It was the last time that he was to see his father, whose health was mysteriously declining. In February 1785 Carlo died at Montpelier of cancer of the stomach at the age of thirty-nine. Napoleon received the news when he had started his course at Paris, while Joseph, as head of the family, was back in Corsica, studying law. Napoleon had been fond of his father, but was stoical in commiserating with his mother:

My dear Mother, Today, when time has calmed a little the first transports of my grief, I hasten to show you the gratitude that your goodness inspires in me. Be consoled, dear Mother, circumstances demand it. We will redouble our care and thankfulness and be happy if by our obedience we can make good a little the boundless loss of a dearly loved husband. I end, my dear Mother, as my sorrow demands, by begging you to calm your own. My health is perfect, and every day I pray that heaven may grant you the same.

At the age of fifteen, he realized that in practice the responsibility of head of the family would devolve on him. He, rather than Joseph, had an assured profession, and he was the more decisive

Napoleon as a student at
Brienne: by Decret.

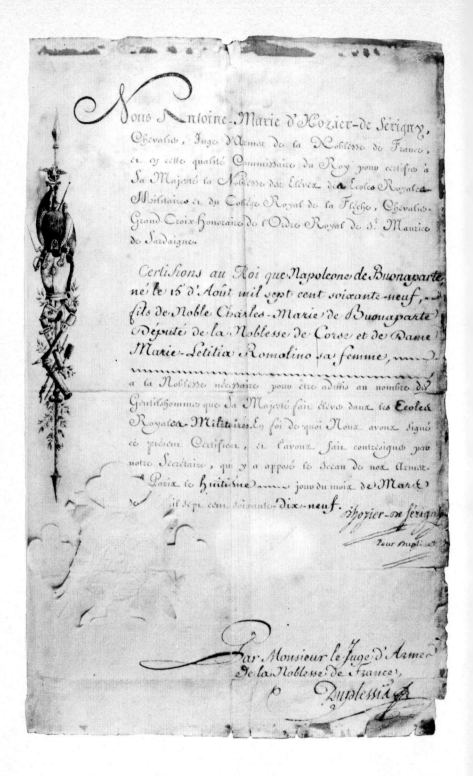

Nous Antoine-Marie d'Hozier de Sérigny,
Chevalier, Juge d'Armes de la Noblesse de France,
et en cette qualité Commissaire du Roy pour certifier à
Sa Majesté la Noblesse des Élèves des Écoles Royales
Militaires et du Collège Royal de la Flèche, Chevalier
Grand-Croix honoraire de l'Ordre Royal de S.t Maurice
de Sardaigne.

Certifions au Roi que Napoleone de Buonaparte
né le 15 d'Août mil sept cent soixante-neuf,
fils de Noble Charles-Marie de Buonaparte
Député de la Noblesse de Corse et de Dame
Marie-Letitia Romolino sa femme,
a la Noblesse nécessaire pour être admis au nombre des
Gentilshommes que Sa Majesté fait élever dans les Écoles
Royales-Militaires. En foi de quoi Nous avons signé
ce présent Certificat, et l'avons fait contresigné par
notre Secrétaire, qui y a apposé le sceau de nos Armes.
à Paris le huitième jour du mois de Mars
mil sept cent soixante-dix-neuf. d'hozier de Sérigny

pour Duplicat

Par Monsieur le Juge d'Armes
de la Noblesse de France,
Duplessis

20

character. The fortunes of the family were sadly confused through Carlo's extravagance and complicated, chimerical schemes. Relying on promises of state-subsidies, he had embarked on two costly schemes of draining a salt-marsh and planting mulberries for the silk-industry. Right up to the Revolution Napoleon was trying to secure these subsidies; but the French exchequer was by now in hopeless disarray, and there was no longer in the government the early enthusiasm for conciliating the Corsicans.

Napoleon spent only one year instead of the normal minimum of two years at the École Militaire. In these circumstances his performance in the passing-out examination was creditable but not notable; he was forty-second on the list of fifty-eight who received commissions. As there were no vacancies in the Navy, Napoleon was clearly destined for the artillery, and he was posted to the artillery regiment of La Fère at Valence in the Rhône valley, on the route to Corsica. With him went Alexandre des Mazis, his closest friend in Paris. Unlike Napoleon he later chose the path of emigration: but when he returned under the amnesty of 1800 he was warmly greeted by Napoleon, and throughout the Empire held a Court appointment as Keeper of the Wardrobe.

Apart from the lavish grants of leave customary in the aristocratic officer corps of the *ancien régime*, the years between 1785 and 1791 which Napoleon spent at Valence or at the artillery school at Auxonne were vitally important in laying the foundations of his success as a professional soldier. The Regiment de la Fère was among the best in the French army, and the commandant at Auxonne was the brother of du Teil who had written in 1778 an important essay on the employment of field artillery and was later to be Napoleon's commander during the siege of Toulon. Moreover, there was the leisure for Napoleon to read widely outside his professional studies. He had literary ambitions and wrote drafts of two romantic novels. Yet despite his increasing involvement in France, his ambitions still remained centred on the family and Corsica. In September 1786 he obtained leave to go home.

He had last been in Ajaccio nearly eight years before. Instead of a Corsican child, his mother was faced with an intellectual young French officer, who could barely talk the Corsican language. His brother Louis, whom he had last seen in the cradle, was now eight, and two sisters and a brother were entirely new to him – six-year-old Maria-Paola, four-year-old Maria-Annunziata (Caroline) and the youngest, Girolamo. Letizia was in such penury that she was

OPPOSITE A certificate attesting to Napoleon's noble birth, a necessary prerequisite for admission to the École Militaire.

reduced to doing all the housework herself. Napoleon rapidly took charge of the family affairs, and in 1787 he visited Paris in a vain attempt to persuade the Paris ministers and bureaucrats to honour their promises made to his father about the mulberry plantation project. It was during this frustrating stay in Paris that Napoleon, as he records in his Memoirs, had his first sexual encounter, with a young prostitute. Napoleon was back in France, at Auxonne, in September 1788 to September 1789, during the outbreak of the Revolution. He had little first-hand experience of those momentous events, beyond suppressing an occasional local food-riot. He and his brother officers took the oath of allegiance to the Nation without difficulty in August 1789. His letters home show that for him the Revolution was primarily an opportunity for Corsica to assert her freedom against French domination. When he again returned to Corsica on leave in September 1789, he found that the island had hardly yet been touched by the Revolution. With the full backing of Letizia, Napoleon threw himself into the activity of organizing a local volunteer National Guard, procuring the election of Joseph as a deputy to the National Assembly and drawing up a petition to the Assembly.

Under the influence of Mirabeau, the National Assembly in Paris took two momentous steps. It proclaimed the integration of Corsica into France, giving the Corsicans all the rights and liberties of Frenchmen; and it invited General Paoli to return from exile as Governor of Corsica. These decisions caused for the Bonaparte family a parting of the ways. It confirmed Napoleon and his brothers in their allegiance to revolutionary France rather than the opposite line of an anti-French policy of resistance.

2 Revolution and Opportunity

Remembering Carlo Buonaparte's defection to the French in 1769, Paoli greeted with some reserve his elder sons Joseph and Napoleon. Joseph was one of the four delegates of Ajaccio to welcome Paoli officially and he also succeeded in being elected as President of the Directory of Ajaccio under the new Constitution. Napoleon passionately defended Paoli in a letter to Buttafoco in January 1791, who had attacked Paoli as a dictator and political charlatan. But it was to be the growing rift between Paoli and the Buonaparte family that was to cut the cord which bound Napoleon to Corsica, and lead to the expulsion and flight of the family. Paoli, during his exile in England and as the friend of Boswell and Samuel Johnson, had become increasingly conservative in outlook; and he would be unable to stomach the growing republicanism and anti-clericalism of revolutionary France.

After obtaining an extension of leave in June 1790, Napoleon finally returned to his regiment in Valence in February 1791, bringing with him his younger brother Louis, aged twelve, to look after his education. Napoleon returned to his intensive course of reading, and also wrote an essay for the prize competition offered by the Academy of Lyons. It received poor marks, and was placed fifteenth in order of merit. As Napoleon recalled at St Helena, 'What ridiculous things I said, how annoyed I would be if they were preserved.' It did survive, and still shows the influence on Napoleon of Rousseau and of Paoli, whom he compares to Lycurgus. There is no trace yet of Napoleon's later terse and individual style.

After a relatively peaceful year in 1790, the Revolution was taking a more critical turn. The King and the royal family made an inept attempt to escape from Paris, and were captured at Varennes, on the way to the eastern frontier and Marie-Antoinette's brother, the Emperor Leopold. Louis xvi's brother the Comte de Provence, the future Louis xviii, escaped without difficulty to Brussels. Marie Antoinette insisted that the whole family should travel together in a large and slow-moving coach, whereas the original plan provided for the King to travel alone in a fast-moving cabriolet. It was the delays on the first stage of the journey from Paris and the incompetence and confusion of the cavalry detachments sent to meet him near the frontier that caused the breakdown of the plan. Drouet, the post master of Varennes, recognized the King, and blocked the road. The citizens and peasantry assembled to prevent his leaving the country. Varennes spelled the death-knell of the monarchy and the approach of war with Europe. A republican demonstration in the Champ de Mars had to be put down by Lafayette and the National Guard by force.

The immediate reaction was a fear of civil war and foreign intervention. The army was put on the alert, and an appeal was made for a hundred thousand volunteers. After a humiliating period of suspension, the King was formally reinstated, but in practice remained a prisoner in the Tuileries. The armed forces were now required to swear an oath to the National Assembly, no longer to the King. Napoleon had no hesitation in taking the anti-monarchical and republican side, and few of the officers of his regiment refused the oath. But a minority, including his friend des Mazis, emigrated in the course of the year.

In September 1791 Napoleon again obtained leave to return to Corsica, as his uncle, the Archdeacon Lucciano, was dying. His death in October, with his legacy of substantial property and cash, brought comparative affluence to the family which enabled them to extend their political activities. In January 1792 the Minister of War granted Napoleon's petition to transfer from the regular army on condition that he obtained election to the post of adjutant to a Corsican volunteer battalion. By rallying his supporters from the countryside, Napoleon secured election as the second Lieutenant-Colonel of the battalion. He found on his return that the political unity of Corsica under the legendary prestige of Paoli was already breaking down, owing chiefly to the anti-clerical measures of the Assembly in Paris involving suppression of monasteries and provoking a schism in the Church. At Easter tension between the factions flared into violence and fighting between Napoleon's national guardsmen and the clericals. Pozzo di Borgo, the royalist and clerical Corsican deputy, denounced Napoleon's actions. Moreover Napoleon had ignored the order from the Ministry of War on the outbreak of war with Austria, that all regular officers should rejoin their regiments by 1 April 1792. If he was to be reinstated in the army list, it was necessary for him to visit Paris. So it happened that he was in Paris from June to September 1792 and was an eye-witness of the fall of the throne in the Revolution of 10 August and of the September Massacres.

Napoleon at the Tuileries on the eve of the fall of the Bourbon monarchy: by Charlet.

It is significant that his letters home at this period reflect an increasing disillusion with revolutionary aims and methods. He describes the Jacobin demonstration and invasion of the Tuileries on 20 June, and concludes that 'It is hard to foresee what will happen to the empire in such circumstances.' Napoleon was reinstated and promoted Captain. There is no description of the events of August and September, and Napoleon abruptly obtained permission to escort his sister Elisa back to Corsica, as her convent school was being shut down. In both Paris and Marseilles she was in real danger of being lynched as an aristocrat.

Moreover, as the King of Savoy had now joined the allies in the war, Napoleon saw the chance of military action from Corsica against the island of Sardinia. At the beginning of 1793 the Paris Government decided on an expedition to capture the off-shore island of Maddalena as a first step to the invasion of Sardinia. Truguet's squadron was sent to Ajaccio with a force of marines from Marseilles, who were to be reinforced by Corsican volunteers. Napoleon was put under the command of Colonna, the second in command of all the National Guards of Corsica. But the expedition in February 1793 was a humiliating fiasco, owing mainly to the indiscipline of the Marseillais and their suspicions of the Corsicans. Napoleon had seized the islet of San Stephano and was reducing Maddalena with his guns, when the Marseillais mutinied and refused to proceed, and the expedition was withdrawn.

It also caused the final breach between Paoli and the French Convention. Already the execution of the King had alienated Paoli from the Revolution. He told Lucien: 'The wretches have guillotined their King, the best of men, a saint. Corsica wants nothing to do with them. It would be better to become Genoese subjects once more. . . . Shame on anyone who sides with the brigands.' It was suspected that Paoli had deliberately sabotaged the expedition, intending to join Sardinia and the British against France. Paoli was summoned to Paris, but refused. On 18 April news arrived in Ajaccio that Paoli had been declared an outlaw and a traitor by the Convention following an address by the Popular Society of Toulon drafted by Lucien, Napoleon's brother. Napoleon was reluctant to provoke a final breach, and published a manifesto defending Paoli; but the Paolists were determined to have done with the Bonapartes and the Jacobins. Paolists in Ajaccio were ordered to capture Napoleon alive or dead, but Letizia was told that no harm would come to her, if she gave written assurance that she disapproved of her sons' action. This she scornfully rejected, and prepared to barricade the house against a siege, with the help of her partisans from the country. Napoleon escaped to Bastia, and sent a message ordering the family to take to the *maquis*, and make for a rendezvous on the coast. In the meantime, Napoleon was making a last effort with a French naval squadron to take the Citadel of Ajaccio. This failed, and he met his mother and the family, who finally sailed from Calvi on 11 June 1793. The Bonaparte house and property were sacked and pillaged, and the family condemned by the Paolist Congress to 'perpetual execration and infamy'. It was the final end of Napoleon's Corsican career and ambitions. Henceforward his duty and the family's lay with France and the Revolution.

The Bonaparte family arrived in Provence as penniless refugees, and moreover at the most critical moment of the Revolution. The treason of Dumouriez and the denunciation of Paoli had been followed by the expulsion of the Girondins from the Convention by the Montagnard Jacobins. The Girondins, in power since the Revolution of 10 August 1792, had provoked war with all Europe, including England, by declaring that the Republic would 'assist all peoples who rise against their rulers'. They had proved themselves incompetent to wage the war they had brought on, and incurred the charge of royalism by resisting the demand for the execution of the King. The Girondins or Federalists raised the Departments against the dictatorship of Paris and fraternized with royalist counter-revolutionaries, with the result that in the summer of 1793 more than half the provinces, and especially the South, were in revolt. But the crisis of the Revolution was also the opportunity for the young professional artillery Captain, when so many officers had emigrated.

The family settled in Marseilles, and were at first dependent solely on Napoleon's army pay, but not for long. Meanwhile the Bonapartes became acquainted with the Clary family, rich textile merchants of Marseilles. Joseph became engaged to the elder daughter, Julie, and they were married the following year, on 1 August 1794. The Convention had promised to provide relief and compensation for the Corsican Jacobin patriots expelled by Paoli, and Joseph hurried off to Paris to expedite the scheme. It never, in fact, matured or produced a single franc. Letizia highly approved a judicious marriage. Julie was far from being a beauty, but she had a loyal and generous character. Above all she was really rich, and her dowry probably exceeded 150,000 francs. Joseph had on his side the fact that he was not only a gentleman but a recognized patriot, with connections in the Convention such as Saliceti the Corsican Jacobin, and was therefore able to protect the Clary family, some of whom had been involved in the Federalist revolt. In his infrequent visits to Marseilles, Napoleon also became interested in the younger Clary daughter, Désirée.

Meanwhile, Lucien, with his typical headstrong egotism, had blotted his copy-book with Letizia and with Napoleon by marrying without even informing the family. From boyhood Lucien had an instinctive dislike of Napoleon and refused to acknowledge his guidance. Even before the family left Corsica, he had written to Joseph:

I tell you in the flood of my confidence that I have always detected in Napoleone an ambition not exactly egoistic, but surpassing in him his love of the public welfare. I really believe that in a free country, he is a dangerous man. He seems to me to be inclined to become a tyrant and I believe that if he was king he would be so, and that his name would be for posterity and for the patriot an object of horror. I see, and it is not merely since today, that in the case of counter-revolution, Napoleone would try to swim with the tide and even, for his fortune, I believe him capable of changing sides.

Employed as a civilian inspector of army supplies at St Maximin in Provence, he had changed his name to Brutus (as was the Jacobin fashion) and married Christine Boyer, the penniless daughter of a local inn-keeper widow. His daughter Charlotte, born the following year, was the first of Letizia's grandchildren.

Napoleon's first action, after settling the family, was to rejoin his regiment at Nice, where he met Jean du Teil, the local artillery commander and brother of his old chief at Auxonne. He was ordered to inspect the coastal batteries. In July he was in Avignon organizing a convoy of gunpowder for the Army of Italy. With time on his hands, he wrote his first effective piece of propaganda, the *Souper de Beaucaire*, which in dialogue form summarized the Jacobin patriotic case against the Federalist rebels. This was published on 29 July, and the revolt reached its most dangerous phase on 27 August when Toulon declared for Louis XVIII and delivered the fleet to the British. At this point chance and luck all fell Napoleon's way. Saliceti, Napoleon's old Corsican friend and patron, was sent south as the deputy on mission to the army

OPPOSITE Lucien Bonaparte: a portrait attributed to Lefèvre. Of the Bonaparte brothers, Lucien was the one least ready to fall in with Napoleon's every wish.

assembling to retake Toulon, and the artillery commander was wounded early in the siege. On 16 September, Saliceti met Napoleon near Nice and offered him the vacant post. Saliceti reported to the Convention, 'Chance has helped us well; we have retained Captain Buonaparte, an experienced officer, who was on his way to the Army of Italy, and ordered him to replace Dommartin.'

In the siege artillery was the dominant arm, and it was up to Napoleon to exploit his luck. With Toulon, he 'enters history'. His army commander, Carteaux, was a Jacobin military ignoramus, whose career had been that of a Court painter. Napoleon was only acting major, but no artillery general arrived until du Teil in November, and he approved all Napoleon's dispositions. From the start Napoleon had seen that the key to Toulon was Fort Éguillette on the western promontory, commanding the passage from the inner to the outer harbour. Once taken, Toulon would be untenable by the British fleet. Napoleon's plan was adopted by the army council, and forwarded to Paris, where it was approved by Carnot. It was not till 14 December that the decisive assault began, which caused the withdrawal of the English fleet, and the fall of the city. Naturally the generals and politicians claimed the credit, but the government was left in no doubt of Napoleon's part. Augustin Robespierre, one of the local deputies and brother of Maximilian, wrote to Paris of this 'artillery officer of transcendent merit'. The concrete reward for Napoleon of all his efforts was his promotion immediately to the rank of Brigadier General, with a salary of 15,000 francs a year. He was able to install Letizia and the family in a country house near Antibes.

Then a fresh turn of the political wheel threw Napoleon's future into jeopardy. In the six months after Toulon, Napoleon had become, under the patronage of Augustin Robespierre, the staff planner of the Army of Italy. When Maximilian Robespierre fell from power and was executed in the *coup* of Thermidor, his brother Augustin went to the guillotine with him; and Napoleon's association with Augustin had been so close that it was inevitable that he should be arrested. He was lucky to escape the guillotine in the White Terror following the fall of the Jacobins, and he probably owed his life to the fact that Saliceti was the deputy in charge of his arrest and examination. He was cleared after a few days' arrest. Lucien had also become too notorious as a Jacobin, at St Maximin, and was also arrested, to be released after strenuous

OPPOSITE Christine Boyer, Lucien's first wife, painted by Gros.

31

The Allied fleets evacuate the port of Toulon, driven out by the French in December 1793: a contemporary engraving. It was now that Napoleon came to the notice of the government, since the strategy employed was his.

efforts by Letizia and Napoleon on his behalf. In the winter, Napoleon was ordered to prepare for an expedition to recapture Corsica. He sailed with the Toulon fleet at the beginning of March, but it sustained such losses in encounter with the British fleet that the project was abandoned. It was only Napoleon's successes in Italy in 1796 that restored Corsica to France and allowed Letizia to return to the family home.

Napoleon now received orders to report to the Army of the West in La Vendée, in command of an infantry brigade. Paoli's alliance with the British had made the employment of any Corsicans in the Army of Italy too suspect. The civil war in La Vendée was the graveyard for military reputations, and Napoleon could only report to Paris, and try to evade the posting. He obtained temporary sick-leave on half-pay, and for a time was depressed, ill and poor. Paris in 1795 was in the grip of appalling war inflation, and Napoleon was kept going only by the help of his faithful aides-de-camp Marmont and Junot, whom he had met at Toulon. He wrote to Joseph, 'If this continues, I shall end by not stepping aside when a carriage rushes past.' He complained that he received no letters from Désirée, and the affair petered out. She was only seventeen, and no doubt the ladies he was beginning to meet in Paris were far more sophisticated and interesting. She was later to marry Bernadotte, and end her career as Queen of Sweden. Napoleon envied Joseph his married state, and even offered marriage to Madame Permon, an old friend of his mother's, whose daughter Laure had called him 'Puss in Boots' when he first wore his lieutenant's uniform on leaving the École Militaire. She later married Junot, and became Duchesse d'Abrantès.

In his depression and impatience, Napoleon thought of professional service abroad. He applied for a posting as artillery adviser to the Sultan of Turkey. His luck, however, was turning, and rapidly. He had one powerful patron in Paris, Barras, who had been one of the deputies on mission at the siege of Toulon, and was now a member of the Committee of Public Safety. Napoleon was temporarily employed in the Topographical Bureau of the Committee of Public Safety, in effect the central military planning department under Carnot. The memoranda he wrote already foreshadow the Italian campaign which he was to put into practice in 1796. In August 1795 he wrote to Joseph, 'Things are quiet here, but storms may be brewing: the primary assemblies meet in a few days.' The latest political crisis was due to the fact that France was

OPPOSITE Desirée Clary, the girl Napoleon had originally hoped to marry. She is seen here in a portrait by Lefèvre painted in 1807 when she was wife of Bernadotte, who became King of Sweden in 1818.

35

being asked to vote on a new Constitution, a return to legality and normality to end the emergency dictatorship of the Committee of Public Safety. After the fall of Robespierre, reaction, counter-revolution and even royalism had gained ground, especially in Paris. To dispose of this threat, and to run no risk of a free vote, the expiring government passed a 'Law of the Two Thirds'. If two-thirds of the new Legislative Council were not members of the outgoing Convention, the places were to be filled by co-option from the Convention. It was unlikely that the Paris Sections would accept this decree without a trial of strength, and they could muster forty thousand men against the eight thousand troops available to defend the Convention.

The key to the crisis lay in the possession and use of the available cannon in or near Paris. In their desperate predicament, the government appointed Barras to command the armed forces, and Barras immediately called in Napoleon to command the artillery. Napoleon sent Captain Murat to fetch forty cannon from the artillery park outside Paris and organized a small, tight perimeter round the Tuileries which could be commanded by cannon-fire. On the following day, 13 Vendémiaire (5 October), the whole fighting lasted a bare hour and a half, and was settled by the 'whiff of grapeshot' from Napoleon's well-sited guns. As the reward for his part in saving the government, Napoleon was immediately promoted to command the Army of the Interior, which carried the rank of full General.

The change in Napoleon's fortunes was startling and sudden, and this time it was not to be a false start. It is not surprising that the bureaux of the War Office were confused about the position of General Buonaparte. As late as 15 September they issued three separate orders. The first struck him off the list of active generals; the second sent him to Turkey; the third put him under the orders of General Buonaparte, in charge of the military mission to Turkey.

It was also through Barras that Napoleon met Joséphine de Beauharnais. She and her friend Theresia Tallien, whose husband had procured Joséphine's release from prison after the fall of Robespierre, were the stars of the Barras 'set', leaders of fashion in the chaotic post-revolutionary Paris. Napoleon comments in a letter to Joseph on the revival of luxury and fashion in Paris, 'This great people is giving itself over to pleasure; dances, theatre, women, and these are the loveliest in the world, are

OPPOSITE Joseph Bonaparte, seen in this engraving wearing the costume of an elector of the Empire.

becoming the rage. Wealth, luxury, good taste, all has come back;
the Terror seems only a dream.' Joséphine contributed the elegance of the *ancien régime*. Born a Tascher de la Pagerie, her branch
of the family had been planters in Martinique since the seven-
teenth century. Married to the even more aristocratic Vicomte
Alexandre de Beauharnais, she was familiar with the Court of
Marie-Antoinette. Soon after the birth of her second child, there
was a separation. Beauharnais embraced the Revolution, and rose
to be President of the National Assembly at the time of the King's
flight to Varennes in 1791 and commander of the Army of the

Rhine in 1793. As aristocrats, he and his wife were caught up in the Terror, and met again in the Carmelite Prison. He was executed on 24 July 1794, and Joséphine just escaped, owing to the fall of Robespierre. She was then a widow with two teenaged children, Eugène and Hortense, and eight years older than Napoleon. Hortense in her Memoirs attests the truth of the story that her brother Eugène, aged fourteen, went to see General Buonaparte after Vendémiaire, when all citizens were ordered to surrender their weapons, to ask that as a favour he might be allowed to keep his father's sword. Napoleon was impressed by

Eugène, granted his request and was thanked by his mother. This may well have begun their real friendship, though he must have met her before in the Barras circle. She was no longer young, and pretty rather than a beauty, but the elegance, grace, gentleness and kindness of her personality have become a part of French history. Napoleon was, to an exceptional degree, sexually inexperienced and naïve in relations with women. Napoleon at St Helena explained that 'My character made me naturally timid in their company. Madame de Beauharnais was the first woman who gave me any degree of confidence.' 'One day when I was sitting next to her at table, she began to pay me all manner of compliments on my military qualities. Her praise intoxicated me. From that moment I confined my conversation to her and never left her side. I was passionately in love with her, and our friends were aware of this long before I ever dared to say a word about it.' He had never been on close terms with a woman of Joséphine's background and charm, and he was soon passionately in love for the first time in his life. Of this there can be no doubt, as the love-letters he sent from Italy in 1796 are some of the most heart-rendingly passionate letters in history. On her side, it was at first no more than yet another amusing affair. By January 1796, she had become Napoleon's mistress. It is sufficient to quote the first of these letters, written in Paris:

I awake full of you. Your picture and the recollection of the intoxicating evening yesterday give my senses no rest. Sweet and incomparable Joséphine, what strange effect do you have on my heart. Are you annoyed? Do I see you sad? Are you uneasy? My soul is broken by sorrow, and there is no repose for your friend. But is there any more rest for me when, yielding to the profound feelings which overcome me, I quench on your lips, on your heart, a flame which burns me. Ah! this night has shown me that your picture is not you! You leave at noon, I shall see you in three hours. Meanwhile, *mio dolce amor*, receive thousands of kisses, but do not return them, for it sets my blood on fire.

OPPOSITE One of Napoleon's love-letters to Joséphine, written while he was on campaign in Italy. His letters prove that his was a genuine passion, though she treated their relationship more flippantly.

The fact that this affair should have turned into a marriage early in March 1796 is less easy to explain. Napoleon did not dare tell his family, and above all his mother, of such an intention. Letizia was bound to react violently against such a choice – a widow with two children, of dubious social and sexual reputation, and above all, of an age which made it unlikely that she could now bear children. For Napoleon, apart from the violence of his passion,

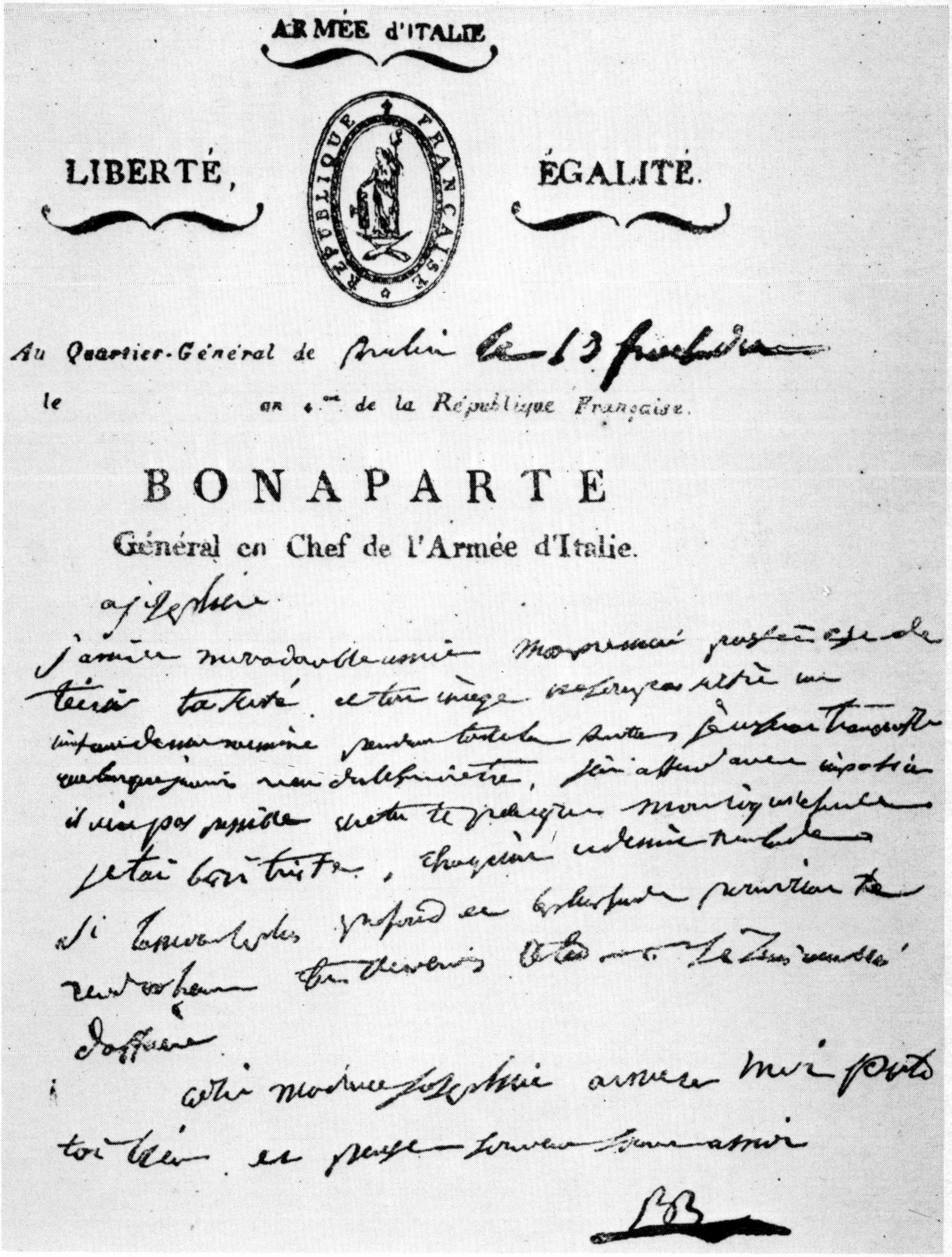
ARMÉE d'ITALIE

LIBERTÉ, ÉGALITÉ.

RÉPUBLIQUE FRANÇAISE

Au Quartier-Général de Milan le 13 fructidor

le an 4.me de la République Française.

BONAPARTE

Général en Chef de l'Armée d'Italie.

a Joséphine

[illegible]

BP

there was the consideration that Joséphine was of impeccable and much higher aristocratic origins than himself and that, on paper at least, the Martinique estates made her potentially wealthy. On her side there was much doubt and hesitation; but her chances of marriage were fading, she was unable to resist Napoleon's determination and she could argue that marriage was now a civil contract, revocable by agreement. The marriage contract suggested a marked degree of independence of the partners. Napoleon settled on his wife the modest sum of fifteen hundred francs. There was to be no community of goods, and Joséphine was to retain custody of her children. If the marriage were dissolved, she would keep all the furniture, clothes, silver and jewels. Napoleon overstated his age by two years, and Joséphine reduced hers by four years, as there were no baptismal certificates available. The notary remarked that 'This man is bringing nothing but his cloak and his sword.' Eight years later, when Napoleon was leaving the Tuileries for his coronation, he sent for the notary and said to him, 'Well, Raguideau, what do you think of my cloak and sword now?'

After Vendémiaire, Napoleon's first thoughts were for his family. On 17 November he wrote to Joseph: 'The family lacks nothing: I have sent them silver, *assignats*, etc. I have just received 400,000 francs for you. I have handed it to Fesch, who will account for it. I may have the family come here.' He procured for Joseph a consular appointment, and for Lucien a post as civil commissioner to the Army of the North. Louis became a Lieutenant, and shortly afterwards aide-de-camp to Napoleon in Italy. Jérôme was sent to school in Paris at Napoleon's expense. Letizia's half-brother, Fesch, became purveyor of supplies to the Army of Italy.

When, at the end of March 1796, Napoleon was appointed to the command of the Army of Italy, Joséphine's connection with Barras, who was now one of the leading members of the executive Directory, started the legend that the Italian command was Napoleon's reward for taking Barras's ex-mistress off his hands. Barras himself asserted this in his Memoirs; but they are unreliable, and the statement was an act of spite and revenge for Barras's expulsion from politics in the *coup d'état* of Brumaire three years later. The Memoirs of another of the five Directors, La Revellière, who had no axe to grind, are more convincing. He confirms that it was a unanimous decision on military and strategic grounds. Carnot, also now a Director, had finally been converted to the project of an Italian offensive, largely by Napoleon's staff memoranda. The elderly commander of the Army of Italy was refusing to move without large reinforcements, and Carnot decided that Napoleon must be given his chance, even if he did not expect very much.

It seems incredible that a man of twenty-six should obtain an independent army command. But there was not only the element of luck and persistence that Napoleon was in Paris to be available for the Topographical Bureau, and the crisis of Vendémiaire; the circumstances of the Revolution, with its wholesale emigration and purging of professional officers, made it probable that a man with Napoleon's rare training and qualifications would, if he avoided emigration or the guillotine, rise rapidly in the Army.

3 Egypt and Brumaire

On his way to the Headquarters of the Army of Italy at Nice, Napoleon stopped briefly to see his mother. He induced her to write a letter to Joséphine; in the circumstances, it was somewhat stilted, formal and disingenuous. 'My son has told me of his happiness, which is enough to ensure not only my consent, but my approval. My own happiness lacks nothing but the pleasure of meeting you. I already consider you one of my children.' Letizia had not only the disappointment of Napoleon's unwise marriage, for she was anxious about Pauline's passionate attachment to Fréron, a journalist already forty years of age, a notorious ex-terrorist and of unsavoury reputation in his private life. With Barras he had been one of the two commissioners of the Convention sent to the South at the time of the siege of Toulon. He had two illegitimate children by an actress. Napoleon was aware that Fréron's terrorist activities would make him out of favour with the new government of the Directory. Napoleon supported Letizia in her opposition, despite and perhaps because of the fact that Pauline was his favourite sister. Pauline wrote sadly to Napoleon, 'You, from whom I expected my happiness, wish me to renounce the only person I can love.'

In the months of April 1796 to January 1797 of Napoleon's astonishing *blitzkrieg* campaign against the Sardinians and Austrians, culminating in the decisive battle of Rivoli, he had little time to spare for looking after the family. All his private thoughts were spent in fretting about Joséphine's delay in joining him in Italy, as shown in his frantic letters to her of this period. She had permission from the Directors to join him in May, but pleaded ill-health as an excuse. Napoleon was delighted at the thought that she might be pregnant, but had suspicions that she had taken a lover. 'It seems to me you have made your choice, and know whom to go to to replace me. I wish you happiness if inconstancy can bring it. I do not say treachery. You have never loved me.' But he did not really believe this, though it was in fact true. With incredible levity Joséphine was openly seeing and was in love with Lieutenant Hippolyte Charles, a young, elegant, worthless hussar on the staff. She even brought him with her when she finally arrived in Italy in the middle of July. Blinded by passion and happiness, Napoleon ignored the existence of Charles.

By April 1797 the Austrians had signed an armistice at Leoben, when Napoleon had advanced within a hundred miles of Vienna. He then lived in vice-regal splendour at the palace of Mombello outside Milan, and summoned the family to join him in enjoying the fruits of victory. 'Never has a military headquarters more closely resembled a Court.' Joseph, Louis and Pauline arrived from Paris; Letizia came from Marseilles accompanied by Elisa, Caroline and Jérôme. Louis, who had fallen mysteriously ill in February 1797, had been unable to complete the campaign of 1797 as aide-de-camp to his brother and had returned to Paris to convalesce. Napoleon's reward was his mother's words when they met: 'Today I am the happiest mother in the world.' But there was never to be peace when the Bonaparte family were gathered together. Secretly the family were already united in a vendetta against Joséphine. Letizia had now to persuade Napoleon to approve the marriage of Elisa to Felix Bacciochi, a noble but undistinguished Corsican captain; Elisa, at the age of twenty, had decided that she must marry soon, or not at all. Napoleon was determined to dispose of Pauline's attachment to Fréron. He struck a bargain with his mother. Elisa should marry her Bacciochi, and Letizia should approve the marriage of Pauline to General Leclerc, one of Napoleon's trusted staff-officers, whom he had known and liked since the days of the siege of Toulon. The poet Arnault, one of Napoleon's staff, draws a picture of Pauline at this time: 'She was at once the prettiest and the most unreasonable person imaginable, with the behaviour of a schoolgirl, laughing at nothing and everything, contradicting the most important people, sticking out her tongue at her sister-in-law behind her back, nudging my knee when I was not paying her enough

Napoleon the victor at the battle of Rivoli in January 1797: a painting by Philippoteaux. Napoleon had completed an astonishingly successful campaign, but Joséphine was still uppermost in his thoughts.

47

attention and attracting to herself the most terrifying looks of reproof from her brother.'

These marriages were celebrated at Mombello, before Letizia departed, after barely a fortnight's stay, to restore her house in Ajaccio. Napoleon procured for Bacciochi the post of military commandant of the citadel of Ajaccio. Some indication of the new wealth of the Bonapartes, coming largely from Napoleon's share of the loot of Italy, is revealed by the dowries of Elisa and Caroline – 40,000 francs from each of the three brothers, Joseph, Napoleon and Louis. Meanwhile Caroline, aged sixteen, had already fallen in love with the dashing Murat. Joseph departed with

LEFT Felix Bacchiochi, the Corsican whom Elisa Bonaparte married: a bust by Chinard. His total incompetence, especially in military matters, was in sharp contrast to his wife's burning ambition.

OPPOSITE General Victor Leclerc, the first husband of Pauline Bonaparte: a portrait by Thibault. Pauline was to lose him on the island of San Domingo in 1792: having subdued the island, he fell victim to an epidemic of yellow fever which wiped out nearly 40,000 inhabitants.

his wife and Caroline to take up the important post of ambassador
in Rome. His mission there was to be brief. After an uprising
against the French, resulting in the death of General Duphot and
an attack on the embassy, the Pope fled from Rome, which became
the Roman Republic.

After his triumphant return to Paris in the winter of 1797 on
completion of the Peace of Campo Formio with Austria,
Napoleon was appointed commander of the 'Army of England'.
England was left as the sole enemy still at war, but Napoleon soon
realized that invasion was impracticable in the face of English sea-
power. He preferred the idea of an expedition to Egypt, which had
already been in his mind before he left Italy, as a result of his
dealings with Venice and Malta.

It was not a new idea. Volney had written in 1788: 'Only one
thing can indemnify France . . . the possession of Egypt. Through
Egypt we shall reach India, we shall re-establish the old route
through Suez, and cause the route by the Cape of Good Hope to
be abandoned.' A former French consul in Egypt had as early as
1795 urged an attack on India by way of Egypt. Arthur Wellesley
had written from India in 1797 that, 'As long as the French have an
establishment in Mauritius, Great Britain cannot call herself safe
in India. They will come here to seek service in the armies of the
native princes, and all Frenchmen in such a situation are equally
dangerous.'

Besides the romantic attraction of this plan, Napoleon was
obsessed with the fear that his reputation would suffer from in-
action in Paris. 'If I remain doing nothing for long I am lost.'

His marriage, already precarious, would be endangered by his
absence. Joséphine would be left to her own indolence, and at the
mercy of the intrigues of the Bonaparte clan. At this time
Joséphine wrote: 'I am so unhappy to be separated from him that
I have a sadness I cannot overcome. On the other hand, his
brother, with whom he corresponds so closely, acts so abomin-
ably towards me that I am always uneasy when I am far from
Bonaparte.' Joseph had warned Napoleon before he left France
that Joséphine and Hippolyte Charles were involved in speculation in army-contracts. There was a bad scene when the two
brothers taxed her with this, and Joséphine then wrote to Charles:
'Yes, my Hippolyte, they have my complete hatred; you alone
have my tenderness and my love; they must see now, as a result of
the terrible state I have been in for several days, how much I abhor

de Hongrie et de Boheme, et la
République françoise, dans l'espace
de trente jours à dater d'aujourd'hui
ou plutôt si faire se peut, et les actes
de ratification en due forme seront
échangés à Rastadt.

Fait et signé à Campo Formio près
d'Udine le dix sept Octobre mil sept
cent quatre vingt dix sept; : vingt-six
Vendémiaire, an six de la République
françoise, une et indivisible.)

Le Marquis de Gallo.   Bonaparte

Louis Comte Cobenzl

Le Comte de Merveldt
Geelhen

Le Baron de Degelmann

Le Directoire exécutif arrête et signe le présent traité de paix
avec sa Majesté l'Empereur et Roi de Hongrie et de Bohême, Négocié
au nom de la République françoise par le Citoyen Bonaparte, Général
en Chef de l'armée d'Italie, fondé de pouvoir du Directoire exécutif et
chargé de ses instructions à cet effet.

Fait au Palais National du Directoire exécutif le cinq Brumaire
an six de la République françoise une et indivisible.

François (de Neufchâteau)   Merlin

them. They can see my disappointment – my despair at not being able to see you as often as I wish.' This is damning evidence of Joséphine's infidelity. But it must be remembered that Napoleon had no intention of being away from France for more than six months at the most. He intended to gain a quick victory over the Mameluke rulers of Egypt, probably in alliance with Turkey, organize the occupation and hand over to a successor. The prospects were suddenly and drastically altered by Nelson's destruction of the French fleet at Aboukir. The expedition was now cut off from France indefinitely, with feeble chances of rescue or reinforcement.

Soon after his arrival in Egypt, Napoleon seems to have become convinced of Joséphine's infidelity, a conclusion he had hitherto evaded. Probably his aide-de-camp Junot had finally told him the fact that Paris knew Charles to be Joséphine's lover. He wrote to Joseph, 'I have great private unhappiness; the veil has at last quite fallen from my eyes.'

At the same time Eugène Beauharnais, now aide-de-camp to Napoleon, wrote to his mother: 'Bonaparte has been extremely sad for five days as the result of an interview with Julien, Junot and Berthier. All I have heard amounts to this that Captain Charles travelled in your carriage until you were within three posting stages of Paris . . . that even now you are with him.' Both these letters were captured by the British cruisers. In October Napoleon told Bourrienne, his Secretary, that he had determined on divorce. Bourrienne describes Napoleon's extreme agitation:

So! I find I cannot depend upon you. These women – Joséphine! If you had loved me you would before now have told me all I have heard from Junot – he is a real friend – Joséphine! – and I six hundred leagues from her – you ought to have told me. That she should have thus deceived me! – Woe to them! – I will exterminate the whole race of fops and puppies! As to her – divorce! Yes divorce! A public and open divorce! I won't write! I know all! It is your fault – you ought to have told me.

In these circumstances, and as a sop to his pride as a cuckolded husband, he acquired a mistress – Pauline Fourès, wife of a lieutenant, who had joined her husband in Egypt. This liaison was public, and it was soon known to the army and to France that Napoleon had a 'Cleopatra'.

Louis returned from Egypt in 1798 with first-hand news of Napoleon's victories. He visited Corsica on his way, told Letizia

OPPOSITE The handle of one of Napoleon's swords which had previously belonged to Francis I and to Charles V: an early nineteenth-century watercolour. The medallion illustrating the battle of the Pyramids was added by Napoleon.

of Napoleon's intention to divorce and persuaded her to visit Paris, as Corsica was now threatened by the British fleet. Thus, in the middle of 1799, the family were assembled in Paris. Joseph had been left by Napoleon in general charge of the family finances, and they had acquired three properties. Joseph bought the country estate of Mortefontaine for 250,000 francs; Lucien bought Plessis for 60,000 francs; Joséphine bought the *château* of Malmaison for 225,000 francs.

Château Malmaison, the home of Joséphine and Napoleon, as seen by the artist Chauvet in 1896.

The news of Napoleon's unexpected and miraculous return from Egypt in October 1799 left the family confident that Joséphine would be repudiated and divorced. Joseph and Lucien, both of whom were members of the Council of Five Hundred, met him on his way to Paris, and gave him the latest news.

Joséphine was also hurrying south to meet Napoleon on the way to Paris; she well knew that the only hope of saving her marriage was to greet Napoleon before he could talk to the

Château de la Malmaison
Façade.

family. But she took the westerly route through Dijon, while Napoleon came through Nevers on the easterly route. Napoleon was for two days in his deserted house, and when Joséphine returned, the bedroom door was locked against her. After a night of mutual anguish, they were reconciled, to the vast disgust of the Bonaparte family, who had been cheated of their prey by the 'Creole'. Laure Junot, later Duchesse d'Abrantès, describes the reactions of the family:

The member of the family who could not endure in silence the pardon given by Bonaparte was Madame Leclerc. She was in a real state of rage. Madame Bonaparte, his mother, was no more content than she was, but at any rate kept quiet. . . . Madame Bacciochi did not restrain herself and did not disguise her contemptuous dislike. . . . As for Caroline she was too young for her opinion to count for anything. As for the brothers they were in a state of open war with Madame Bonaparte and did not hide it.

The reconciliation was outwardly complete; Joséphine never saw Charles again, and Pauline Fourès was pensioned off. But there was a price to be paid: it was now Napoleon who had grown cynical, and felt himself entitled to conduct affairs with other women as he chose, while Joséphine never took another risk, and became more and more terrified of losing Napoleon.

It was the news from Europe that had made Napoleon decide to return, risking capture by the British cruisers. He learned that Russia and Austria had joined Britain in the Second Coalition, that all his Italian conquests had been lost and southern France threatened with invasion, and that an Anglo-Russian expedition had landed in Holland. Clearly the crisis had come which might bring him to supreme power in France, and the Army of Egypt could be saved only by victory in Europe. All the way to Paris he was received with hysterical acclaim. Hortense, who accompanied Joséphine on her journey to meet Napoleon, recalled that:

Whenever we stopped to change horses crowds pressed round the carriage and asked if it were true that their 'saviour' had arrived, for that was what all France was calling him now. With Italy lost, the treasury bankrupt, the Government devoid of both strength and reputation, Napoleon's return seemed a blessing from heaven. The journey from Fréjus to Paris was a series of triumphs that showed both him and his enemies what France wanted of him.

The disastrous position of the Egyptian expedition was obscured by the news of Napoleon's last crushing victory over the Turkish invasion at Aboukir. In Paris he found that preparations for a *coup d'état* against the discredited government was far advanced, and he was courted by each faction. The Directory, which Napoleon had helped to put into power at the crisis of Vendémiaire, had not done well, either at home or abroad. The strict division of power between the executive Directory and the Legislative Councils ensured that they were never in agreement, and discord could be overcome only by an unconstitutional purge. In Fructidor (September) 1797 Napoleon had sent Augereau to Paris to carry out a purge of the Directory, and the Constitution had never recovered respect. Secondly, the government had inherited a fearful problem of inflation of the paper-money (the *assignats*) from the Convention. They had repudiated the debt and the paper-money and tried to return to a metallic currency, but the administrative machine was not strong enough to ensure the collection of taxes. They were propped up by the exactions from occupied territories, as in Italy, but when these were lost, the situation became uncontrollable. Bands of brigands were fed by deserters from the armies who could not be paid. The royalist civil war in the west flared up again. The deficit on the budget for 1799 amounted to 400 million francs.

Nelson's annihilation of the French fleet in the battle of the Nile had led to the formation of the Second Coalition against France. First Turkey, then Naples, followed by Russia and Austria, joined in the Second Coalition. In April 1799 an Austro-Russian army under Suvorov had occupied Milan, and on 15 August Joubert, the new commander of the Army of Italy, had been defeated and killed at the battle of Novi. In March Jourdan's Army of the Danube had been defeated at Stockach. The situation had to some extent been stabilized, as Masséna defeated the Russians at Zürich (16 September) and Brune had forced the Duke of York's expeditionary force in Holland to re-embark (18 October). The Second Coalition was to prove more fragile than it appeared. Bernadotte and Jourdan were associated with the Jacobins in the Council of Five Hundred, who were clamouring for a return to the Terror. They passed a Law of Hostages, authorizing the imprisonment of relations of *émigrés*, and an income tax which alarmed the financiers and the middle classes. On 14 September, a motion to declare the 'country in danger' (which meant a return to revolutionary dictatorship) was narrowly defeated in the Council

OVERLEAF The battle of Aboukir, July 1799: the painting is by Lejeune. Here, Napoleon inflicted a crushing defeat on the Turks, driving most of them into the sea.

Victoire d'Aboukir en Égypte, le 7 thé. an
Bonaparte Général en Chef.

of Five Hundred. The moderates rallied and succeeded in carrying the elections of the Presidents of the Councils. The President of the Council of Five Hundred was Napoleon's brother Lucien. Bernadotte was dismissed from the Ministry of War.

Sieyès, the new Director and leader of the moderates, had been looking round for a 'sword' to play the part which Augereau had filled in the *coup* of Fructidor. He had thought of Joubert, and after his death, Moreau, who was hesitant. When Moreau heard of Napoleon's arrival in the south of France, he told Sieyès, 'There is your man, he will create your *coup d'état* better than I.'

The Jacobins would offer him a military dictatorship and a return to the Terror. Barras needed his support to remain in power: Sieyès, the New Director, led the moderate bourgeois faction who wished to defeat the Jacobins and strengthen the executive power. Napoleon had no intention of being a prisoner of a faction; he soon chose Sieyès, reckoning that in the event he would be able to control and discard him. It was essential to act quickly, and Napoleon had little to do with the planning of the ill-prepared and bungled procedure of the *coup*.

It was this situation which brought Lucien, now in the key position of President of the Council of Five Hundred, to the fore, and made his part in the *coup* crucial. On paper, the whole operation should go through without difficulty. The Generals, with the exception of Bernadotte, Jourdan and Augereau, would follow Napoleon. The two key regiments were commanded by Sebastiani, a Corsican comrade of Napoleon in the Italian campaign, and by Murat; Sieyès and Ducos would manage the remaining Directors and the Elders. Lucien was in the key position of President of the Five Hundred. Fouché, as Minister of Police, would hold the ring. On the first day, 18 Brumaire, all went smoothly. The Council of Elders voted for a special session of the Councils at St Cloud, outside Paris, and appointed Napoleon commander of the Paris troops. Barras and two other Directors, not in the plot, were induced to resign.

The weak point in Sieyès's procedure was the delay in the meeting of the Councils, and in the preparation of the halls at St Cloud. It gave too much time for the Jacobin opposition in the Councils to mobilize. Sieyès was nervous about their activities, and suggested to Napoleon that forty of them should be arrested. Napoleon rejected this proposal, saying, 'I do not fear such feeble enemies.' The session did not open till after mid-day, and by

3.30 pm Napoleon in his impatience appeared before the Elders, and made a confused and threatening speech which created the worst impression. He concluded by an appeal to the military: 'If there is talk of declaring me *hors la loi*, I shall appeal to you my brave companions in arms. Remember that I march accompanied by the god of victory and the god of fortune.' He then entered the hall of the Five Hundred alone and, before he could speak, was physically attacked by angry deputies. It was now that Lucien by his presence of mind and improvisation saved the day. As President he resisted all attempts to vote 'outlawry and treason' against Napoleon. Then he and Napoleon appeared on horseback before the Guards of the Councils, and Lucien's speech won them over. 'The President of the Council of Five Hundred declares to you that the great majority of the Council is at this moment terrorized by certain deputies armed with daggers.' He added that 'these brigands' were 'doubtless in the pay of England'. This was enough to send the troops in, and the deputies fled. Later that night a rump of the Councils voted for the nomination of a provisional executive of Sieyès, Ducos and Napoleon. A semblance of legality was just, but only just, preserved.

In the following day's bulletin there was no mention of Lucien's part in the affair; but he got his reward in his appointment as Minister of the Interior. Joseph and Joséphine had also contributed to the success of the *coup* by their extensive friendships with the leading moderate politicians. Joseph was nominated one of the commissioners to negotiate a peace-treaty with the USA. Louis received exceptional promotion to the rank of brigadier-general. Murat was now permitted to marry Caroline Bonaparte. He had distinguished himself exceptionally in the battle of Aboukir and in the proceedings of 19 Brumaire at St Cloud. Napoleon had thought of marrying Caroline to General Moreau, but he withdrew his objections when it was clear that Moreau had already a fiancée and married in November 1800. Murat was appointed commander of the new Consular Guard.

It was in the debates with Sieyès behind the scenes that the basis of Napoleon's dictatorship was laid. Instead of Sieyès's plan for a Grand Elector and two equal Consuls, Napoleon insisted on a First Consul with full powers of decision, the Second and Third Consuls being merely consultative. But even when the Constitution was promulgated in January 1800, the new régime remained on trial. It was not till after the victory of Marengo in Italy that the

autocracy of Napoleon was confirmed. After the Concordat with the Pope and the conclusion of the Peace of Amiens, Napoleon was made Consul for life instead of for ten years, and possessed in practice the powers of an absolute monarch.

When in 1804 the Consulate was transformed into a hereditary Empire, it was not merely the result of Napoleon's personal ambition; there was a general desire among the classes which had benefited from the Revolution for security for their gains. The peasants feared that a restoration of the monarchy would mean the loss of the national lands they had purchased – the lands of the Church and of the *émigrés*. The ex-revolutionary regicides would be in danger. Soon after Brumaire the King in exile –

Louis XVIII – had written to Napoleon proposing a restoration of the monarchy, and had been definitively rebuffed.

Assassination plots increased the sense of insecurity and demands for the solution of a hereditary succession. On 24 December 1800, Napoleon and Joséphine were due to visit the opera for a first performance of Haydn's Oratorio *The Creation*. There was a violent explosion in the Rue Niçaise which Napoleon escaped by seconds, largely because his coachman, who was frequently drunk, was driving very fast. Joséphine, Caroline and Hortense in the following carriage were slightly hurt by broken glass. The explosion came from a cart carrying a wine-barrel filled with gunpowder, and nine people were killed and twenty-six injured. Napoleon insisted that it was a Jacobin plot but Fouché had good evidence that it was the work of the Vendéan royalist Georges Cadoudal.

The British Government had throughout the Revolution maintained a royalist fifth column. Not content with the failure in the Rue Niçaise, Cadoudal put up a plan for 'kidnapping' the First Consul. This plan was revived after the renewal of war in 1803. Cadoudal and his men were landed in the Pas de Calais by a British naval officer, Captain Wright, in August 1803. Fouché had a double agent who informed him that not only Cadoudal but an exiled republican general turned royalist, Pichegru, were in France and that Pichegru was meeting General Moreau. A Bourbon prince was expected to follow shortly. The police were alerted, and in February 1804 it was announced that not only Moreau but Pichegru, Cadoudal and twenty other royalists had been arrested in Paris. Cadoudal and nineteen other conspirators were condemned to death, but of these eight members of the *noblesse* were reprieved, owing partly to the pleading of Joséphine on their behalf.

It was at first thought that the Bourbon prince could be the Comte d'Artois, and the Channel ports were under close surveillance. Then attention was turned to the Duc d'Enghien, grandson of the Prince de Condé, who was living just across the Rhine in Baden. There was evidence that in the event of a Continental war, he was to lead an *émigré* force into Alsace. Napoleon ordered that he should be seized, despite the neutrality of the territory of Baden. His papers showed no connection with the Cadoudal plot; nevertheless, Napoleon ordered his trial by court-martial, and he was shot at Vincennes without the opportunity of an appeal, under a law of 1791 relating to *émigré* conspiracy. Joséphine implored Napoleon for mercy, but he replied, 'You wish to see me murdered.' Even in his Will at St Helena, Napoleon defended his action: 'I had the Duc d'Enghien arrested and tried because it was necessary for the safety, interests and honour of the French people, at a time when the Comte d'Artois openly admitted that he had sixty paid assassins in Paris. In like circumstances, I should do so again.' There were three motives in Napoleon's mind. Firstly it was an act of collateral vendetta in the Corsican tradition. Secondly, his violent act of retaliation had the desired effect: it ended royalist plots against Napoleon's life. Lastly, by shedding Bourbon blood, Napoleon made himself an accomplice of the regicides and ex-Jacobins, and removed any doubt about a restoration of the monarchy. In prison Cadoudal remarked, 'We have done more than we hoped to do; we wanted to give France a King, and we have given her an Emperor.'

On 18 May 1804, the Senate declared that, subject to ratification by plebiscite, 'The Government of the Republic is entrusted to a hereditary Emperor.'

4 The Empire and Hereditary Succession

As Napoleon's personal power grew, the question of the succession became a matter of desperate intrigue within the family. It was an issue which was to bedevil family relations till the end of the Empire. Joséphine was terrified by the question: as it became less and less likely that she would bear a child, she was threatened by the danger of a divorce. To counter this, she even encouraged rumours that the sterility of the marriage was not her fault, but Napoleon's. The brothers were insistent that their 'rights' should be safeguarded and recognized. As early as 1801, an anonymous pamphlet was distributed from Lucien's office of the Interior, entitled *Parallèle entre César, Cromwell, Monk et Bonaparte*. It contained passages which openly posed the question of heredity: 'The fate of a great man is subject to greater hazards than that of ordinary men. New discords! Return of calamities! If suddenly Bonaparte was lost to the Nation, where are the heirs?' It was clearly the work of Lucien, and Napoleon was furious at this initiative. He deprived Lucien of the Ministry of Interior, in which he had in any case been a failure, and sent him off to Madrid as Ambassador, where he could console himself by amassing a large fortune. In fact he returned from Madrid after six months with a million francs, a collection of valuable paintings and a Spanish mistress. His wife, Christine, had died in childbirth in 1801. On his return Lucien was restored to favour and nominated to the Tribunate. Napoleon recognized him as the ablest of his brothers, but the most independent and unpredictable. He now proceeded to blot his copy-book finally by falling in love with, and marrying,

Alexandrine Jouberthon. She was of bourgeois origin, was married to a stockbroker and had two children. Her husband had become bankrupt, and left for San Domingo to repair his fortune. Although Lucien had no proofs of his death in San Domingo, he contracted a secret religious marriage when his son by Alexandrine was born, and later a public civil marriage. Napoleon was annoyed by this *mésalliance* which contravened the principles he had carefully written into the Code Civil, and refused to recognize Alexandrine as a member of the family. This Lucien refused to accept, and retired to Italy. He wrote to Joseph, 'I depart with hate in my heart.' Napoleon could not contemplate Joseph as his heir; he was too idle and lacked firmness and competence. He chose Louis, blinded by his affection for his obedient younger brother, and unaware of the dangerous development of Louis's ill-health, melancholia and paranoia. It is probable that Louis had contracted syphilis at Milan in the Italian campaign, and he now suffered from permanent ill-health. Napoleon thought it was temporary, and could be cured by a change of scene. As soon as Joséphine became aware of Napoleon's design, she thought of a marriage between Louis and Hortense, as a means of bridging the gap between the Bonapartes and the Beauharnais, and of strengthening her own position.

Hortense de Beauharnais, like her brother, co-operated with a good will in her mother's plans to keep relationships with the Bonapartes sweet, and as a result made a disastrously unhappy marriage with Louis.

OPPOSITE Hortense seen in a self-portrait.

LEFT Hortense as Queen of Holland, with her children: detail from a drawing by Prud'hon.

67

In September 1801, Louis returned from travel in Germany and became engaged to Hortense at a ball at Malmaison. There seems no doubt that at this stage he was genuinely in love with Hortense. She had been passingly in love with Colonel Duroc, one of Napoleon's greatest friends and later to be Grand Marshal of the Imperial Household, but she was happy to fall in with her mother's wishes. They were married in January 1802. The wedding was the occasion of vile rumours which infiltrated the English Press that the marriage had been hurried on because there had been an incestuous relationship between Napoleon and Hortense. Napoleon treated Eugène and Hortense as if they were his own children; there is no foundation for the sinister rumour.

Equally silly were the periodic rumours that Napoleon's love for Pauline was incestuous. Pauline had accompanied her husband Leclerc who had been nominated as commander-in-chief of the expedition to reconquer San Domingo, during the period of peace with England. Leclerc was at first brilliantly successful, and the Negro leader Toussaint l'Ouverture was sent back as a prisoner to France. Then the deadly yellow fever struck and practically wiped out the army. Leclerc himself died of it and Pauline returned with his body, heart-broken and seriously ill. During the recovery, Prince Camillo Borghese, one of the richest men in Europe, happened to be in Paris. Borghese had no objection to marrying a Bonaparte, and Pauline saw attractions in the title of Princess and the Borghese riches and diamonds. No difficulties were raised by Napoleon, who in pursuance of the Concordat and his Italian plans welcomed the idea of alliance with a Roman prince. Pauline, however, angered Napoleon by a secret marriage with Borghese before the time prescribed for widows, and he refused to attend the official wedding.

Napoleon, irritated by Jérôme's extravagance as a young man in Paris, insisted that he should prepare for a naval career. He was cruising in the Caribbean when the rupture with England was imminent in 1803, and his Admiral decided that it was safer for him to return to France in a neutral ship. This gave Jérôme an excuse to visit the United States, where the French were still extremely popular, and where the brother of the First Consul would be lionized. At Baltimore he met the beautiful Elizabeth Patterson, daughter of a wealthy and leading merchant of the city. They fell in love, and Betsy was entranced at the idea of escaping from Baltimore, which was too narrow for her ambitions, to Europe.

The French Consul-General was in despair when he knew of Jérôme's intention to marry, and pointed out that under the Code Civil he could not marry without his parents' consent till he was twenty-five. Jérôme defied the warning, but he and his bride could not reach Europe till April 1805, owing to the British blockade. By this time Napoleon had become Emperor and issued orders that the woman accompanying Jérôme was not to be

Betsy Patterson, first wife of Jérôme Bonaparte: a portrait by Gilbert Stuart. This determined American beauty and her father were shrewd enough to procure an agreement whereby Jérôme should make over to her a third of his fortune if the marriage were annulled. Pensioned off, she dismissed her connection with the Bonapartes thus: 'Had I waited, with my beauty and wit, I would have married an English Duke, instead of which I married a Corsican blackguard.'

ABOVE A portrait of Pauline by F. G. Kinson.

LEFT Prince Camillo Borghese, Pauline Bonaparte's second husband: a portrait by Gérard.
Pauline characteristically soon grew bored with him, and spent much energy in publicly
humiliating him, devoting her attentions to a series of unsuitable lovers, before they
finally separated.

admitted to the Empire. Jérôme was ordered to proceed to Milan to report to the Emperor, who was about to be crowned as King of Italy. He refused to see Jérôme until he had submitted to his conditions. After days of agonizing indecision, Jérôme yielded, and Napoleon wrote to him: 'Your union with Miss Patterson is null in religion as in law. Write to her and tell her to return to America. I will grant her a pension of 60,000 francs during her life on condition that in no event she shall bear my name, to which she has no right, her marriage being non-existent.' Betsy returned to America, but it was by no means the last that the Bonaparte family heard of her. (In 1807, Jérôme was made King of Westphalia in pursuance of Napoleon's European policy and agreed to marry Catherine, daughter of the Duke of Württemberg.) So now all the brothers and sisters were married, for better or worse.

In the Constitution of the Life-Consulate in 1802 and that of the Empire in 1804, Napoleon outmanœuvred his brothers by resorting to the Roman practice of adoption of an heir. Napoleon said to Roederer, a friend and adviser of Joseph:

You forget that my brothers are nothing except through me, that they are great only because I have made them great, and the French people know them only through the things I have said of them. There are thousands of persons in France who have performed for the State more services than they: you yourself are one of them. I will not tolerate that they are put beside me on the same level. The system which prevails also does not allow it. When I departed for Egypt, I left all my wealth with Joseph, he has never rendered an account, but I have become too great to bother about that. He has been the friend of my childhood. I do not wish that he should complain about me at any time. But one must look facts in the face. Joseph is not destined to rule; he is older than me. I should outlive him, I am in good health. Moreover he was not born in a rank sufficiently elevated to be plausible. I was born in poverty: he was born like me in extreme obscurity. I have raised myself by my actions. He has remained at the point where birth placed him. To rule in France, one must be born in grandeur, be seen since childhood in a palace with guards, or else be a man capable of distinguishing himself above everybody else. I have never accepted that my brothers should be the natural inheritors of power. I have considered them as men appropriate to preserve power from falling at the first chance during a minority. It is only on this basis that they have been nominated in the Senatus Consultum. Hereditary succession to succeed must pass to children born in grandeur. If he has a son, I could adopt one. I will not be unjust to him but his wife does not produce

sons any more than mine. You must present him only as an intermediary appropriate in certain eventualities to ensure the succession of my family. The French people have not voted anything for him.

In a final interview with Joseph, Napoleon delivered an ultimatum:

I have reflected much about the dispute which has arisen between us, and I will tell you first that in the week this quarrel has lasted I have not had an instant of repose. I have lost sleep on it, and you are the only person who could exert such an influence on me. I know of no event which could trouble me to this point. You have the choice of three courses: firstly to resign and retire from public life, renounce everything. Secondly to continue to enjoy the rank of a French prince and nevertheless remain, as you have up to now, in opposition to my system. Thirdly, to unite yourself frankly with me, and become, let us say it, my first subject. . . . The third course is the simplest, the one which suits you best and which you must finally adopt. Place yourself in a hereditary monarchy and be my first subject. It is a sufficiently important position to be the second man in France and perhaps in Europe. . . . I am destined to change the face of the world: that is my belief. Put yourself then in a hereditary monarchical system where so many advantages are promised to you. Carry out my wishes, follow my ideas. Do not flatter the patriots when I repel them. Do not turn your back on the nobles when I summon them. In a word, be a prince and do not be afraid of the consequences of this title. When you succeed me, you can return to your favourite ideas. I shall be no more.

In 1802 Napoleon was given the right of nominating his successor. The proposal emanated from Joseph and Lucien, and it was extremely unwelcome to Napoleon, as it would be impossible to avoid nominating Joseph. At first he regretted the proposal by the Council of State. Joseph explained to his confidants that:

You do not understand my brother. The idea of sharing his power enrages him so much that my ambition is as suspect to him as that of anyone else, perhaps more, because it is the most plausible of any that might appear and more justifiable to general opinion. He wishes above all that the need for him should be felt acutely and that his existence should be such a great benefit that nothing can be envisaged beyond it without fear. He knows and feels that he rules by this idea more than by force or gratitude. If tomorrow, one day, one could say 'there is a stable and tranquil order, here is a successor who will maintain it', there will be no trouble to fear, my brother would no longer believe in his safety. Such is the feeling that I detect it in him; such is the unalterable rule of his conduct.

However, Napoleon yielded in the Constitution of the Life-Consulate and was given the right of nominating his successor but swiftly shelved the question by taking no action.

In 1804 the hereditary succession of the children of his brothers was established, but only after the adoptive heir. Napoleon was given the right to adopt a son of his brothers, provided he had reached the age of eighteen. Unofficially he announced his intention of adopting Napoleon-Charles, the eldest son of Louis and Hortense. Imperial princes could not marry without the approval of the Emperor. The Constitution of the hereditary empire was therefore a mixture of the Roman practice of adoption, and of

Louis, King of Holland, with one of his sons: a portrait by Wicar. Napoleon had said of Louis: 'I can easily see that he will turn out a better fellow than any of the four of us,' a prediction which fell sadly short of fulfilment, but nevertheless it was Louis's eldest son whom Napoleon selected as his adoptive heir.

strict hereditary right subject to the French principle of the Salic Law excluding females from the succession. Both Joseph and Louis were very angry and protested against their 'rights' being passed over, but in the end they yielded; Joseph accepted the position of Grand Elector, and Louis that of Constable and Chief of the Imperial Guard. Bacciochi was made a Senator, and Murat, already a Marshal, was made High Admiral of France. Lucien and Jérôme did not share in the honours, and were not designated as Imperial Highnesses, because they were in disgrace over their marriages. Elisa and Caroline were furious when they discovered that they were not to be Imperial Highnesses, while Pauline was a Princess in her own right. They would remain plain Madame Bacciochi and Madame Murat, while the wives of Joseph and Louis, who were not Bonapartes, would be 'Princesses'. It was, of course, logical according to French custom, by which women enjoyed no rank of their own, but only that of their husbands. There was a terrible scene between Napoleon and Caroline which ended in Caroline fainting and Napoleon yielding. In the course of the row, Napoleon exclaimed: 'To hear you talk, one would think I had stolen from you the inheritance of our late father' – a concise comment on the relations of Napoleon with his family. At this time Napoleon complained to a confidant, Roederer, that:

They're jealous of my wife, of Eugène, of Hortense, of everybody around me. Joseph's daughters don't even know yet that I am called Emperor – they call me Consul. Whereas little Napoleon, when he goes past the grenadiers in the garden shouts to them 'Long live Nonon the soldier.' I love Hortense, . . . if Hortense asked to see me when I was in council, I would go out to her. If Madame Murat asked for me I would not. With her I always have to take up positions for a pitched battle: to make a young woman of my own family understand my point of view, I have to endure speeches as long as I would to the Senate or the Council of State. They say my wife is untrustworthy and her children's attentions insincere. Well, I like them; they treat me like an old uncle; that sweetens my life. I'm growing old, I'm thirty-six. I want some peace and quiet.

The day after, the *Moniteur* announced that the 'French princes are given the title of Imperial Highness. The sisters of the Emperor take the same title.' Letizia, absent in Italy, was worried and affronted by her own position. Her step-brother Fesch wrote to Napoleon:

OPPOSITE *Madame Mère*: a portrait by Gérard. She is seated by a bust of Napoleon crowned with laurels as Emperor of the French. Throughout the drama of Napoleon's rise to fame, this formidable mother was involved in the fortunes of all her family, and like them concerned about her own position in the new hierarchy.

Your mother has departed for the waters of Lucca. Her health is undermined more by moral afflictions than physical handicaps. I have noticed that her illness increases every time she sees the courier arrive without letters for her. Her desolation was extreme when she learned from the gazettes the elevation of your Majesty to the Empire: she has been extremely affected at not receiving any courier during the three months she has spent at Rome. She imagines that your Imperial Majesty prefers any other member of the family to herself. These melancholy reflections penalize her strong constitution, cancel all the good she might hope for from the journey, the climate and the remedies. I have done everything for her, I have neglected nothing to calm her and make her stay in Rome agreeable, but all my efforts have been defeated by the grave illness of Madame Clary who is so delicate.

Your mother desires a title, a stable position. She is disturbed by the fact that some call her Majesty, Empress, Mother, while others give her only the title of Imperial Highness as for her daughters. She is impatient to know that her status has been fixed. She does not wish to return to Rome. She hopes that Your Majesty will call her to Paris before the end of August, the date of her departure from Lucca.

Napoleon applied his mind to the problem; the difficulty was that there was no precedent for the mother of a sovereign who had not herself been a Queen. Eventually it was solved by giving her the title of '*Altesse Impériale, Madame, Mère de l'Empereur*', and henceforth she was unofficially known as '*Madame Mère*'. But Napoleon took care to withhold her title, until she had agreed to refuse recognition of Jérôme's marriage with Betsy Patterson.

There were more battles over the ceremonial of the Coronation, which Napoleon himself meticulously worked out. He rejected the first idea of an open air ceremony, and the Church of the Invalides as it was too small. It had to be in Nôtre Dame, and extensive works were required for both the interior and the exterior. Isabey the painter was in charge of the costumes, and Napoleon chose as his personal emblem, to replace the *fleur-de-lys*, the bee found in the tomb of the Merovingian King Chilperic. New crowns and regalia were commissioned from the Paris jewellers. As the Pope had finally accepted Napoleon's invitation, the Coronation had to be delayed till 2 December. Napoleon was determined that Joséphine should be crowned, though there was no precedent for a French Queen being crowned since Marie de Médicis. As Napoleon said to Roederer, 'I am above all a just man. If I had been thrown into prison instead of ascending a throne, she would have shared my misfortune. It is right for her to share my grandeur.' But there were certain difficulties involved. The Pope insisted that there should be a religious ceremony of marriage before the Coronation, as he would not recognize the civil marriage of the Directory. Joseph at first threatened to absent himself, if Joséphine were crowned. Napoleon wanted his sisters to carry the train of the Empress, but they violently protested against this 'indignity'. They capitulated when Napoleon delivered an ultimatum – do as I say or do not attend the Coronation. Their susceptibilities were smoothed by a compromise which stated that the Princesses were to 'support' the mantle of the Empress rather than to 'carry the train'. *Madame Mère* still delayed her return from Italy, hoping for a reconciliation with Lucien. She was not in fact present at the Coronation, and the inclusion of her portrait in David's great picture of the Coronation is historically inaccurate. The malicious Pauline vented her feelings against Joséphine by giving a violent tug on her sister-in-law's train so that she nearly fell backwards as she moved towards the altar to be crowned by Napoleon. It was a freezing cold day on 2 December, but everything on the whole went smoothly. It had been agreed beforehand between the Pope and Napoleon that the Pope should anoint the Emperor, but that Napoleon should crown himself. The Coronation cost at least eight million francs, and the Pope received more enthusiasm from the populace than did Napoleon. It was for him a further big step towards the counter-Revolution.

As Napoleon was President of the Italian Republic, the proclamation of the Empire entailed a change of the Italian Republic to a kingdom. Napoleon was due to be crowned King of Italy in Milan in May 1805. But he saw an opportunity of conciliating Joseph, disposing of his claims as Napoleon's heir-apparent and at the same time reassuring Austria. He proposed that Joseph should accept the crown of Lombardy, with the promise that the crowns of France and Italy should never be united. If Napoleon died before he could adopt an heir at the age of eighteen, then Joseph was to succeed him, and Louis was to have Italy. Joseph at first appeared to accept this proposal, then, after delay, refused. Napoleon then turned to Louis, and proposed that his son Napoleon-Charles should have the kingdom of Italy, with Napoleon as Regent until he came of age. Louis refused to give up his right in favour of his son. At the cost of increasing the tension with Austria, Napoleon fell back on the scheme of making Eugène Beauharnais

OVERLEAF David's well-known painting of the imperial coronation: Napoleon is portrayed crowning Joséphine. Two of his sisters are shown carrying the Empress's train and *Madame Mère* is included for artistic purposes.

81

his Viceroy in Italy, though he was aged only twenty-four and inexperienced in government. At the same time he made Elisa Princess of Piombino and Lucca: Bacciochi received no right of sovereignty, only the empty title of Prince of Lucca. It was a convenient way of getting rid of the awkward Bacciochi, and Elisa was to prove an effective Bonaparte administrator.

Napoleon had succeeded in shelving, but not solving, the question of the succession. He had now other things to think about, as his assumption of the crown of Italy was the final provocation which led Austria to ally with Russia and England in the war of the Third Coalition. Napoleon's brilliant successes in this war brought about the creation of the Grand Empire, and elevated the Bonaparte family to new and undreamed-of heights of splendour, if not of power.

OPPOSITE David's sketch for his coronation painting, showing Napoleon crowning himself, with his back to the Pope.

5 Austerlitz and the Grand Empire

The peace with England, and the Continental peace, did not last long. Even before the Preliminaries of London were confirmed by the Peace of Amiens, English public opinion was turning against it. Malmesbury commented, 'Peace in a week, war in a month.'

In signing the Peace of Amiens, the British Government assumed that the *status quo* in Europe would be maintained. They soon found that Napoleon was delaying the evacuation of Holland, and intervening by the Act of Mediation in Switzerland (February 1803). In Italy he had annexed Piedmont, Elba and Parma, and transformed the Cisalpine Republic into the Italian Republic, of which he was President. In Germany, as the result of the Treaty of Lunéville of 1802, which ended the Continental war, the Holy Roman Empire was dissolved, and many of the free cities and ecclesiastical principalities were annexed by the south German states which now looked to France rather than to Austria.

There were hopes that peace would bring a revival of the free trade commercial treaty of 1786, but they were soon disappointed. Napoleon made it clear that he intended to exclude English goods from the whole coastline under his control. This was a policy that he had inherited from the Convention and the Directory, and he was in a position to make it more effective. The 1786 Treaty had been very unpopular in France and was associated with the outbreak of the Revolution. After an initial boom, English exports began to decline at the end of 1802 as Napoleon's policy of prohibition began to bite. There were fears in England of renewed

French colonial competition, aroused by the San Domingo expedition and the purchase of Louisiana from Spain. Peace, or rather the 'cold war', was proving very advantageous to France. At St Helena Napoleon said: 'At Amiens I believed, in perfectly good faith, that my future and that of France was fixed. I was going to devote myself solely to the administration of France, and I believe that I should have performed miracles. I would have made the moral conquest of Europe, as I was on the point of achieving it by force of arms.'

It would have needed immense restraint to halt the expansion of France at this point; a restraint which was totally foreign to Napoleon's character. As Vandal says, 'It is impossible to say whether the task was beyond the capacity of his genius; it was certainly beyond the capacity of his character.'

The French ambassador in London explained the reason for the British dislike of the peace: 'It is not such and such a fact but the totality of facts comprising the First Consul's *gloire* and the greatness of France that frightens the English.' They might have been prepared to acquiesce in the French possession of Belgium, provided that French expansion went no further. What was impossible for the British government to accept was an overthrow of the balance of power in Europe and a French hegemony of the Continent. A power which dominated the Continent could organize the ship-building resources of Europe and challenge English sea-power. As Napoleon himself said to his Minister of Marine, 'It will take us at least ten years; after that time, with the help of Spain and Holland, we may perhaps hope to challenge the power of Great Britain with some chance of success.'

Pitt, although no longer in office, advised that Malta should be retained as compensation for the French gains in Europe since Amiens. Diplomatically this was a poor case, as the *status quo* in Europe was guaranteed not by the Peace of Amiens but by the Treaty of Lunéville, to which Britain was not a party.

Lord Whitworth, full of anti-French and anti-Bonaparte prejudice, was appointed ambassador in Paris and told to say nothing about the evacuation of Malta. He sent home ludicrous judgments on the situation in France, describing Napoleon as a 'duplicate of Tsar Paul' and opining that 'France was ripe for revolt'. Napoleon tried to put pressure on Britain to evacuate Malta by publishing a report by General Sebastiani that 'Six thousand men would suffice to reconquer Egypt.' The British Cabinet seized on this as an

Napoleon presents medals of the Légion d'Honneur for the first time in the church of Les Invalides, on 15 July 1803: a painting by Debret. He had created the Légion d'Honneur the year before.

excuse to declare that Malta would not be given up unless the *status quo* of 1801 was restored. After a violent scene between Napoleon and Whitworth in the presence of the other ambassadors, Whitworth finally left Paris in May 1803, despite the fact that Napoleon offered to accept Russian mediation in the dispute.

There seems to be no doubt that between 1803 and 1805 Napoleon seriously intended to invade England, though later he claimed that it was a blind in order to train the Grand Army for use against Europe. At its peak, the Boulogne flotilla aimed at a total of two thousand boats to transport a hundred thousand men. He soon dropped the idea of invasion by the flotilla alone, and aimed at temporary command of the Channel by the battle-fleet. In December 1804 Spain entered the war on the French side, and Napoleon elaborated his 'grand design' by which Villeneuve should sail for the West Indies, thus forcing the British to disperse in defence of the West Indies. Villeneuve would then return with temporary command of the Channel. It did succeed in luring Nelson to the West Indies, but he did not deceive Barham at the Admiralty into abandoning concentration of force.

Villeneuve never dared to come north after returning to Europe, and took refuge in Cadiz. So the scene was set for the battle of Trafalgar in October 1805. But in the meantime Napoleon had abandoned the invasion project at the end of August 1805, and switched his forces to the Danube.

Pitt had succeeded in forming a third Continental coalition against France. Prussia persisted in her policy of selfish neutrality and hoped to get Hanover with French help. Tsar Alexander I wavered throughout his reign between a western policy of rivalry with Napoleon and an eastern policy of isolation and partition of Turkey. At the beginning of his reign his advisers were strongly anglophile, and he was jealous of Napoleon's increasing influence in Germany and his designs on the Near East. In April 1805 an Anglo-Russian Convention was signed which aimed at the liberation of the territories acquired by Napoleon since the Peace of Amiens. If the war was successful, Belgium was to be united to an independent Holland, and Genoa given to a restored Piedmont. In August 1805 the Third Coalition crystallized when Austria was finally provoked by Napoleon's coronation as King of Italy in Milan. This, and the annexation of Genoa, were a clear breach of the Treaty of Lunéville, and seemed to portend the exclusion of Austria from Italy.

The Allies assumed that Italy would, as before, be the main theatre of war. The Archduke Charles in Venetia was given eighty thousand men while Mack in Germany had only sixty thousand men. Napoleon put Masséna in command in Italy with forty thousand men. Mack completely underestimated the speed of Napoleon's advance. He calculated that Napoleon would arrive with seventy thousand men, and could not reach the Danube in less than eighty days, by which time the Russian advance-guard

would have joined the Austrians. In fact Napoleon was across the Rhine by the end of September with 190,000 men. He had also summoned south Bernadotte's corps of observation in Hanover. Mack, before he had fully grasped the danger, was surrounded at Ulm and forced to capitulate with fifty thousand men on 20 October 1805.

Kutusov was now in command of the Austro-Russian forces and evaded Napoleon's pursuit, but Vienna was abandoned to

The eve of the battle of Austerlitz (December 1805), one of Napoleon's most stunning victories, movingly described by Tolstoy and painted here by a contemporary artist.

Napoleon on 14 November. He was now in the depths of Moravia with long lines of communication and much wastage. Kutusov's reinforcement had brought his army up to ninety thousand men, and the Archduke Charles was falling back. If Prussia now joined the Allies, Napoleon would be in great danger. Tsar Alexander had persuaded Frederick William III to sign a Potsdam Convention on 3 November, but he insisted on sending an envoy to Napoleon with an ultimatum which did not expire till 15 December. As Tsar Alexander had now arrived at allied Headquarters to assume command, Napoleon was straining every nerve and using every ruse to tempt him into a decisive battle as soon as possible.

Alexander's aide-de-camp Prince Dolgorouki had an interview with Napoleon on 30 November, and reported that Napoleon was weak and could be defeated. Napoleon manœuvred as if to retreat, and tempted the allied army into stretching their line to bar the retreat of his right wing. As soon as Napoleon saw that the centre of the allied position, the heights of Pratzen, had been weakened, he sent in a powerful thrust, and cut the allied army in two. The battle of Austerlitz ended in the most decisive of all Napoleon's victories. The French casualties did not exceed eight thousand, and the allied losses in killed, wounded and prisoners were twenty-seven thousand men. The Emperor Francis sued for an immediate armistice, and Alexander withdrew to Russia much shaken and demoralized. The Prussians signed a treaty with Napoleon in Vienna, receiving Hanover in return for Anspach and Neuchâtel.

With the death of Pitt in January 1806, Fox came into office and attempted a general peace negotiation. This goaded Prussia into a suicidal war with Napoleon, after missing the favourable opportunity in 1805. But peace would certainly mean the return of Hanover to Britain, and Prussia had sacrificed everything for the bait of Hanover. As late as August 1806 Napoleon was giving orders for the Grand Army to withdraw from south Germany, but they were cancelled on 3 September, and Napoleon was at his headquarters in Bamberg when he received the Prussian ultimatum on 7 October. The Prussian striking-force of 130,000 men was not inferior to the French, but it was an antiquated army which had learned nothing since Frederick the Great took the field. With a high proportion of foreign mercenaries, rigid discipline, slow moving baggage-trains, elderly generals and an ill-educated officer-corps, it was no match for the Grand Army at the

OPPOSITE Napoleon with the Emperor of Austria after the battle of Austerlitz: a sketch by Prud'hon.

OVERLEAF Napoleon arrives at the field of battle at Jena, in October 1806: a contemporary print. He scored another victory here, his cavalry chasing the fleeing Prussians through the city.

An engraving published in 1806 celebrating the victories of Napoleon over the armies of Austria and Russia in Germany. It was dedicated to the Emperor's Minister of War, Alexandre Berthier.

peak of its efficiency and morale, and the result could only be a foregone conclusion.

In the two battles of Jena and Auerstadt fought on 14 October, the Prussian army was virtually destroyed, and Murat's relentless cavalry pursuit completed the rout. By 25 October the French were in Berlin, and Frederick William had taken refuge in Königsberg.

It now appeared that Russia was intending to fight in Poland. Napoleon raised a Polish contingent of thirty thousand men by hints of independence for Poland, and undertook a difficult winter campaign. There was an indecisive battle at the end of the year at Pultusk, and in February 1807 a surprise attack by the Russians on the scattered French forces led to the battle of Eylau. It was extremely costly in casualties, and the first major check for Napoleon. If Austria took advantage of the situation, he would again be in a precarious position, but Austria was too shaken by the defeat of Austerlitz to recover. By the spring of 1807, new conscripts had increased the strength of the Grand Army, and on

14 June Napoleon gained his decisive victory over the Russians. The Russian commander Bennigsen moved his army across the River Alle assuming that he had only a French advance guard to deal with. Napoleon was able to arrive in time with the bulk of his forces, and the bridges were set on fire. The Russian army was crushed against the river. Napoleon wrote to Joséphine that 'The battle is as decisive as Austerlitz, Marengo and Jena.' The Tsar had for some time been depressed by the isolationist attitude of England and the feebleness of Prussia, and he now readily made peace in the Treaty of Tilsit – perhaps the high watermark of Napoleon's European career.

Napoleon is invited to dine with the Tsar and other members of the Russian imperial family at Tilsit: a contemporary print.

These enormous successes left vast territories and whole kingdoms at the disposal of Napoleon, and created the Grand Empire in addition to the French Empire of 1804. His first plan – and it was obvious and inevitable to a man of his Corsican feeling of family responsibility regardless of its efficiency – was to create federated states around France, ruled by members of his family.

Maria-Carolina, the Austrian wife of Ferdinand of Naples and sister of Marie-Antoinette, had double-crossed Napoleon in the war of 1805. Having made a treaty with France in the autumn of 1805, she secretly encouraged an Anglo-Russian force to land in southern Italy. It hurriedly withdrew when the news of Austerlitz arrived. Napoleon had determined to oust the Bourbons from the Kingdom of the Two Sicilies, and sent Masséna with a strong force to occupy Naples. At the same time he ordered Joseph to join Masséna as nominal commander-in-chief. In March 1806 Joseph was proclaimed King of the Two Sicilies (though the Bourbons still held Sicily, protected by the British fleet). This time Napoleon made no attempt to force Joseph to give up his rights in France; it was specifically stated that he remained Grand Elector of France, and retained his rights to the succession.

The principality of Guastalla was given to Pauline, and Louis was made King of Holland in 1806. He was already known to the Dutch as he had commanded the Army of the North based on Antwerp during the campaign of 1805. In February 1806, Napoleon offered the Dutch the choice of annexation to France or a monarchy under his brother. They chose the latter as it might preserve some independence. Louis protested that he would rather rule at Genoa or Turin, but yielded to the will of Napoleon.

Murat had greatly distinguished himself as a cavalry leader in 1805, and in 1806 he and Caroline were rewarded with the duchy of Cleves and Berg, with the capital at Düsseldorf. Henceforward, Murat was Prince and Grand Duke, and Caroline was temporarily appeased.

Jérôme, after further service at sea, had been promoted to the rank of Rear-Admiral at the age of twenty-two, and in 1806 he was attached to the Grand Army to gain military experience. He was being groomed for a new kingdom, which was created in 1807, that of Westphalia, composed of territories taken from Brunswick, Hanover, Hesse-Cassel and Prussia, with a population of two millions and a capital at Cassel. Jérôme also agreed to marry Catherine, daughter of the Duke of Württemberg.

OPPOSITE Joachim Murat, the handsome and feckless husband of Caroline: detail from Gros's painting of the battle of Eylau. Unfaithful to each other, the couple also betrayed Napoleon in 1814. The Emperor described him as 'a brave man on the battlefield, but feebler than a woman or a monk when the enemy is not in sight. He has no moral courage.'

In 1806 Eugène de Beauharnais was married to Augusta, daughter of the Elector (now King) of Bavaria, who had been Napoleon's ally in 1805. Eugène was now given the titles of Imperial Highness and 'son of France'. The Beauharnais scored another victory when Eugène's cousin Stephanie married the Grand Duke of Baden, who had originally intended to marry Augusta of Bavaria. Murat unwisely criticised the Bavarian marriage in a letter to Napoleon:

When France raised you to the throne it was because she thought to find in you a chief of the people, a plebeian chief, endowed with a title which raised you above all the sovereigns of Europe, but it was not her intention to recreate the monarchy of Louis XIV with all its abuses and all the pretensions of the old courts. Yet you surround yourself with the old nobility, you fill the salons of the Tuileries with them, they believe themselves restored to all their rights; they consider themselves more at home than they think you are. The old nobility considers all your comrades in arms, and perhaps even you yourself, as intruders, and usurpers. Today you intend by the marriage of Eugène to ally yourself to the royal House of Bavaria, and all that you are doing is to show to Europe how much value you put on that in which we are all lacking: the prestige of birth.

Lucien remained unavailable to Napoleon's federal system. Elisa wrote realistically to Lucien in June 1807: 'One cannot deal with the master of the world as an equal. Nature made us children of the same father and his prodigious feats have made us his subjects. Though we are sovereigns, we hold everything from him.' Lucien was confirmed in his resistance to divorce by the approval of the Pope who consented to be godfather of his latest child, and recognized the validity of the marriage. At the end of 1807 Napoleon paid a visit to Italy, and met Lucien at Mantua. Napoleon remained adamant that divorce of his wife was the price of Lucien's recognition as a French prince and that of his daughters as French princesses, and Lucien remained equally firm that he would not divorce. Napoleon wrote to Joseph:

I have seen Lucien at Mantua. I have talked with him for several hours; no doubt he has told you the disposition in which he left. His thoughts and his language are so distant from mine that I have difficulty in knowing what he wanted. It seems to me that he said he wished to send his eldest daughter to Paris to her grandmother. If he sticks to this disposition, I wish to be told of it immediately, and it is necessary that the young person should be at Paris in the course of January, either

OPPOSITE Eugène de Beauharnais, of whom Napoleon said: 'He never caused me any strife.' The portrait is by an unknown artist. The loyalty of Joséphine's children to Napoleon was perhaps equalled only by that of *Madame Mére.*

accompanied by Lucien, or whether he commissions a governess to take her to Madame. Lucien appeared to me to be torn by different feelings and not to have the will-power to make a choice. All the same, I can tell you that I am ready to give him the rights of a French prince, to recognize all his daughters as my nieces, provided that he begins by annulling his marriage with Madame Jouberthon, either by divorce, or some other means. This done, his children will be established. . . . You will see that I have exhausted all means in my power to recall Lucien (who is still in his first youth) to the employment of his talents for me and for the country. I do not see what he actually alleges against this system. The interests of his children are covered; I have provided for everything. Once the divorce has gone through, and Lucien is established elsewhere, with Madame Jouberthon having a grand title at Naples or elsewhere, if Lucien wishes her to join him, provided it is not in France; if he wishes to live with her in whatever intimacy he wishes, I shall not create any obstacle, for it is the political aspect which alone is my concern. Given that, I do not wish to contest his tastes or passions. Such are my proposals. If he wishes to send me his daughter, she must leave without delay and in reply he must send me a declaration that his daughter is leaving for Paris and that he puts her entirely in my charge. There is not a moment to lose; events are moving and it is necessary that my destiny should be fulfilled. If he has changed his mind, I must know it also immediately, for I will make other dispositions, disappointing though it will be, for why should I not recognize these two young nieces who have nothing to do with the complication of passions of which they should not be the victims. Tell Lucien that his grief and the sentiments that he showed me have touched me and that I regret all the more that he will not be reasonable and contribute to his repose and mine. I await with impatience a clear and definite reply, particularly as concerns Lolotte.

No reconciliation was possible, and the only outcome of the talks was a project that Lucien's daughter Charlotte should visit Paris. Napoleon envisaged the possibility that Charlotte, aged twelve, should marry the Crown Prince of Spain, Prince of the Asturias, or that he might even marry her himself.

When Charlotte arrived in Paris to stay with her grandmother, she wrote home malicious gossip about the family which, intercepted by the censor, scandalized and amused Napoleon. She had to be packed off home. It is not too much to say that her disappearance may have profoundly affected Napoleon's relations with Spain. If she had married the Prince of the Asturias, Napoleon's disastrous error of dethroning the Spanish Bourbons would have been averted. Lucien may therefore indirectly but substantially have contributed to the fall of the Empire. In 1809, when the Pope was evicted from Rome, Lucien decided to escape altogether from his brother's domination and emigrate to America. The American ship in which he embarked with his family was driven by storms into Sardinia and fell into the hands of the British fleet. After detention at Malta, Lucien was conveyed in a British frigate to England, and detained. He was allowed to purchase an estate in Worcestershire, where he lived the life of a wealthy country squire at Thorngrove. Much of his time was spent in composing a bad epic poem on Charlemagne.

The circumstances of the campaign of 1806–7 were fatal to Joséphine's future. In the Polish campaign of the winter of 1806 Napoleon met the beautiful Marie Walewska, wife of an elderly Polish nobleman. Napoleon fell passionately in love with her, and her friends persuaded her that it was her patriotic duty not to resist his advances. While Napoleon enjoyed the company of Marie Walewska at Finkenstein, he was writing to Joséphine with excuses to prevent her from joining him in Poland. In the spring of 1807, Napoleon-Charles, the young son of Louis, tragically died. The death of the destined adoptive heir, of whom Napoleon had been very fond, increased the constant rumours of a divorce, and the consolidation of Napoleon's power required that he should form a marriage alliance with one of the European dynasties. Fouché, the powerful Minister of Police, openly broached the necessity of a divorce to Joséphine. In the campaign of 1809 Marie Walewska joined Napoleon at Vienna, and by the autumn she was pregnant, and Napoleon had no doubts that he was the father. Already a previous mistress, Eléonore Denuelle, to whom he had been introduced by Caroline, had had a son, probably by Napoleon, possibly by Murat. The news of the birth of this son, later known as the Comte Léon, reached Napoleon in Poland on the last day of 1806. In 1807 Napoleon began to draw up lists of eligible European princesses, and Joséphine wrote to her children on the question of divorce. Eugène wisely advised her in reply: 'He must treat you well, give you an adequate settlement and let you live in Italy with your children. The Emperor will then be able to make the marriage which his policy and his happiness demand. . . . If the Emperor wishes to have children who are truly his, there is no other way.' The fragility of the succession was borne in on Napoleon when he discovered an intrigue by Caroline, Talleyrand and Fouché to promote Murat as his successor in

case of Napoleon's death in the campaign of the winter of 1808 in Spain. Napoleon was warned by Eugène who intercepted a message from Talleyrand to Caroline, and he returned in haste to Paris. Talleyrand was disgraced, and ceased to be Foreign Minister. Now there could be no doubt that Napoleon was capable of producing children, and from this moment Joséphine's divorce became only a matter of time.

On his return from Vienna he did not resume marital relations, and on 30 November 1809 at a *tête-à-tête* dinner with Joséphine, he broke the news that he was determined on a divorce. This was confirmed in a meeting with Joséphine and Eugène, and followed by a formal family council at which a *senatus consultum* dissolving the marriage was drafted. The religious marriage was dealt with by the French ecclesiastical authorities in default of the Pope. She was to retain the title of Empress, with an allowance of three million francs, and she kept Malmaison in full ownership, and the Elysée for her lifetime.

The eligible princesses were now reduced to three – Anna, the younger sister of the Tsar, a Saxon princess and the elder daughter of the Emperor Francis of Austria, Marie-Louise. On his return from Vienna, Napoleon sent a formal offer to St Petersburg for the hand of Anna. But he had not much hope of a favourable reply, as the Dowager Empress, a fanatical enemy of Napoleon, had the final say, and in his meeting with Tsar Alexander at Erfurt in 1808, he had shown himself lukewarm and evasive about the Tilsit alliance. On the other hand, the House of Habsburg was the grandest dynasty in Europe, and Napoleon had been impressed by the toughness of the Austrian resistance in the Wagram campaign. Moreover there had been a disturbing attempt to assassinate him at Vienna. In the course of a review at Schönbrunn, a young German tried to present a petition. A general was suspicious of his manner and had him arrested. A large knife was found on him. Napoleon, in an interview with him, cross-examined him about his intentions, hoping that he would prove to be insane. But he reiterated his intention to kill Napoleon as a tyrant and oppressor of the German people. Hitherto Napoleon had had to fear assassination only by Bourbon agents, and he was deeply concerned to find that a middle-class student who ought to welcome the enlightenment of Napoleonic rule, should wish to kill him. There was a new spirit stirring in Europe.

Countess Metternich was in Paris to urge the Austrian marriage

OPPOSITE Marie Walewska, Napoleon's second great love: an unfinished portrait by Gérard. She remained true to Napoleon, visiting him in exile with their son Alexandre.

The marriage of Napoleon and Marie-Louise: painted by Rouget. This marriage of convenience produced an heir, but Marie-Louise's loyalty to the Emperor did not survive their separation, when he was exiled.

to forestall Russia. The reply from Russia was a veiled refusal – Anna's fate could not be settled till she was two years older, eighteen. Napoleon settled immediately for the Austrian match and Countess Metternich wrote to her husband, 'Now the affair is successful and all that we could desire.' Berthier was sent to Vienna to arrange the marriage by proxy which took place on 11 March, with the Archduke Charles taking the part of the bridegroom. Caroline was sent to meet Marie-Louise on her journey and bring her to Compiègne. Napoleon did not wait for the civil wedding in order to consummate the marriage. In November 1810 it was announced that the Empress Marie-Louise was pregnant, and in March 1811 a son was born, the King of Rome.

OPPOSITE Marie-Louise and the King of Rome: painted by Gérard. The portrait confirms descriptions of her pink and blonde looks.

6 The Satellite Sovereigns

Napoleon at St Helena recalled that 'My family have not helped me.' At St Helena he said, 'Joseph loved pleasure and women too much. Lucien, a bad subject. Lucien had no principles. He wanted to marry the Queen of Etruria and a few days later to marry Madame Récamier.' The system of satellite kingdoms planned by Napoleon after Austerlitz did not work out well, because there was a basic misunderstanding. His brothers thought of themselves as independent sovereigns linked to France by treaty, whereas Napoleon thought of them as his prefects to carry out his will without argument.

Eugène was certainly exempted from this criticism; throughout the Empire he acted as the loyal, efficient and uncomplaining Viceroy in Italy. His head was not turned, as well it might have been, by his marriage with the Bavarian Crown Princess and his formal recognition as Napoleon's adoptive son and heir presumptive to the crown of Italy in default of male heirs to the Emperor. His arranged marriage had turned out to be a love-match, and for this he was deeply grateful to his step-father. Writing to Joséphine about the birth of his son in March 1811, Napoleon added: 'I am always quite satisfied with Eugène. He has never caused me the slightest sorrow.' In 1807 he told a friend: 'My present position sometimes seems to me like a dream. In the midst of all my splendours I sometimes long to return to my independence in Paris – the days when I was with my regiment. But, as regards the Emperor, I have only one course – obedience.' When he was summoned to Paris in the winter of 1810 for the formalities of

The imperial women in the Bonaparte family, with the King of Rome shown in the centre: a contemporary print.

Joséphine's divorce, Eugène asked Napoleon's leave to retire from Italy, but was persuaded to remain. Of course, his wife was disappointed by the Austrian marriage. It meant that her children were deprived of a crown. But neither she nor Eugène harboured a grudge.

In view of his youth and inexperience, Eugène was at the start closely supervised by Napoleon, who deluged him with letters of advice. He had also a powerful and efficient bureaucracy to support him, headed by Prina, the Minister of Finance. Melzi, created Duke of Lodi, retired to the post of the Keeper of the Seals. Prina succeeded in balancing the budget until 1814, despite the strains and dislocation imposed by the Continental System. The kingdom of Italy supplied France with raw materials such as cereals and silk, and in return was a profitable market for French manufacturers. The system of licences eased the ban on English goods, and there was extensive smuggling. In 1810 a large quantity of silk went to Illyria and thence to Malta.

As a professional soldier, Eugène proved himself to be a fine organizer and trainer of troops. A mere twenty-three thousand in

De tout quoi a été dressé le Présent Procès Verbal auquel Sa Majesté l'Empereur et Roi Napoléon; et Son Altesse Impériale et Royale l'archiduchesse Marie Louise ont apposé leurs signatures; et qui après avoir été Signé par les Rois, Reines, Princes et Princesses presens, ci dessus Nommés été Signé par Nous, et Contresigné par le Secrétaire de l'Etat de la Maison Impériale qui l'a Redigé.

fait au Palais Imperial de S. Cloud, les jour, heure, et an susdits.

A document signed by Napoleon and Marie-Louise, Louis, Jérôme, Borghese, Murat and Eugène.

1805, the Italian army rose through the application of conscription to forty-four thousand in 1808, and a maximum of ninety thousand in 1813. Twenty-seven thousand served in Russia in 1812, and twenty-eight thousand in Germany in 1813. The Italian corps fought with distinction and was practically destroyed in Russia.

In 1805 he was subordinate to Masséna, commanding in northern Italy. In the 1809 campaign, Eugène led an Italian corps to join Napoleon at Vienna for the decisive battle of Wagram, winning on the way a battle at Raab in Hungary. In 1812 he was given the command of the 4th Corps of eighty thousand men, including besides his Italians, two French divisions, the Bavarians and the reserve cavalry. The formation of the Italian army and bureaucracy and the abolition of feudalism through the application of the Code Napoleon inevitably, and contrary to Napoleon's intentions, promoted a feeling of Italian unity and nationalism. It was to be the ex-officers and civil servants of the Empire who led the first stages of the Risorgimento after 1815. Eugène himself, if not exactly popular as the representative of a foreign dynasty, was highly respected in Milan.

Joseph and the French army were well received at Naples in 1806, largely because of the hatred felt for Maria-Carolina. Calabria was rapidly pacified, though the fortress of Gaeta held out for the Bourbons, and the British from Sicily landed six thousand men in Calabria, under Stuart, who defeated Reynier at Maida. They then withdrew leaving a garrison at Reggio.

From the first, Napoleon and Joseph differed in their conception of the new kingdom. Napoleon regarded it as conquered territory, and wanted Frenchmen in all the key-positions and as a new aristocracy. Joseph wanted to retain his initial popularity by governing a native government of Italians; he regarded himself as the legitimate successor of the Bourbons 'by the grace of God'. Like Eugène, Joseph was supported by some key French bureaucrats, Miot, Roederer and Saliceti. Marshal Jourdan, a competent professional, supervised the army. Indignantly Napoleon found himself forced to pay for the forty-five thousand French troops needed to keep order, and to send Joseph subsidies amounting to six million francs. He complained that 'Naples cost me a lot of money and deprives me of an army.' But it was of strategic importance, and Napoleon was secretly impressed by the example that Joseph was giving of enlightened and liberal government.

OVERLEAF The battle of Wagram, July 1809: by Rugendas. A less spectacular victory than that of Austerlitz, Wagram concluded Napoleon's last successful campaign.

In his short reign, Joseph made a considerable start in the abolition of feudalism, reform of the tax-system and encouragement of education and the arts. He even made some progress with the development of a native Neapolitan army, despite the hatred of conscription and a high rate of desertion. Brigandage, ending in Calabria, was put down by the French army of occupation. His success, however, was due to his brilliant subordinates and ministers. He was too indolent and too fond of easy popularity to be a good administrator on the model of his brother.

Joseph made no attempt to persuade his wife, Julie, to join him in Naples, nor had she any desire to leave Mortefontaine. Only in March 1808 did she leave for Naples on the direct orders of Napoleon. Meanwhile Joseph maintained a brilliant Court and numerous mistresses.

Elisa earned her promotion as Grand Duchess of Tuscany in 1809 by hard work and good administration. In her letters to Napoleon, she always took trouble to treat him as a pupil to her master, and as a subject to her sovereign. She fostered the industries of Lucca, and the marble industry of Carrara. Education and the arts were developed, and her Court was renowned for its musical and theatrical distinction. Paganini was her Court musician (and also her lover). The amiable Bacciochi was content to be a figurehead, excluded from government.

Pauline had no political ambitions. Her health since the San Domingo expedition had been precarious, and she spent much time in taking cures at watering-places. Subject to her health, she lived for society and pleasure, and was content to obey her brother. In 1809, after her formal separation from Prince Camillo Borghese, Napoleon gave her the *château* of Neuilly and an allowance of 600,000 francs. She was now a rich woman, with an income of a million francs, and was able to entertain on a scale which she considered suitable for the Emperor's sister. Her sexual appetite was notorious and insatiable, and her doctors were seriously concerned that her health would be permanently damaged by the success of her affair with the handsome officer Auguste de Forbin.

Louis considered that he had been freely invited by the Dutch delegation to become King, and he intended to follow a Dutch policy. In his first speech he said, 'Your principles are mine . . . you have the right to a Dutch King. From this day begins the true independence of the United Provinces.' Thus, in contrast to the other satellite states, his ministers were all Dutch patriots. Louis was so sensitive to Dutch feeling that he was slow in implementing the Napoleonic reforms. It took two and a half years to pass a heavily revised Code Napoleon. It was particularly irritating to Napoleon that Louis refused to introduce conscription, and consequently was never able to raise the quota of troops for foreign service which Napoleon considered appropriate. In the critical campaign of 1809 and the English landing at Walcheren, Louis failed to raise more than twenty thousand troops and it was left to the French to oppose the English expedition.

Holland was in debt when Louis arrived, and less than a year after his arrival, the Berlin decree establishing the Continental System was fatal to the Dutch economy, which depended on overseas trade. The most serious friction between Napoleon and Louis arose on the latter's refusal and inability to apply the Continental System effectively.

The breakdown of the marriage between Louis and Hortense caused Napoleon concern. He wrote to Louis:

Your quarrels with the Queen are known to the public. Show in your private life the paternal and soft side of your character, and in your administration the sternness you display at home. You treat your young wife as though she were a regiment. You have the best and worthiest wife in the world, and yet you are making her unhappy. Let her dance as much as she likes, she is just the age for it. Do you expect a wife of twenty who sees her life slipping away, and dreams of all she is missing, to live in a nunnery or a nursery, with nothing to do but bath her baby? Make Hortense happy as she is the mother of your children. The only way is to treat her with all possible trust and respect. It's a pity she is so virtuous – if you were married to a flirt, she would lead you by the nose. But she is proud to be your wife and is pained and repelled by the new idea that you may be thinking poorly of her.

By 1809 Napoleon had concluded that Louis must go, and a first sign of this decision was his offer of the Grand Duchy of Berg to the elder son. It obviously meant that he would not inherit Holland. After his return from Wagram, Napoleon started a campaign of open propaganda against the failure and treachery of Holland in applying the Continental System. In March 1810 Louis was so exasperated and depressed that he announced his abdication in favour of his elder son, 'convinced that I am an obstacle to the return of good feelings between my brother and the country'. Napoleon ignored the terms of the abdication and proceeded to annex Holland to France. Louis retired to Toplitz in

OVERLEAF Elisa Bonaparte surrounded by dignitaries: by Benvenuti. Elisa had pretensions as a *saloniste*, but usually had to draw people into her circle through the good offices of Madame Récamier. However, in time David, Gros and Isabey were among those to be found at her salon.

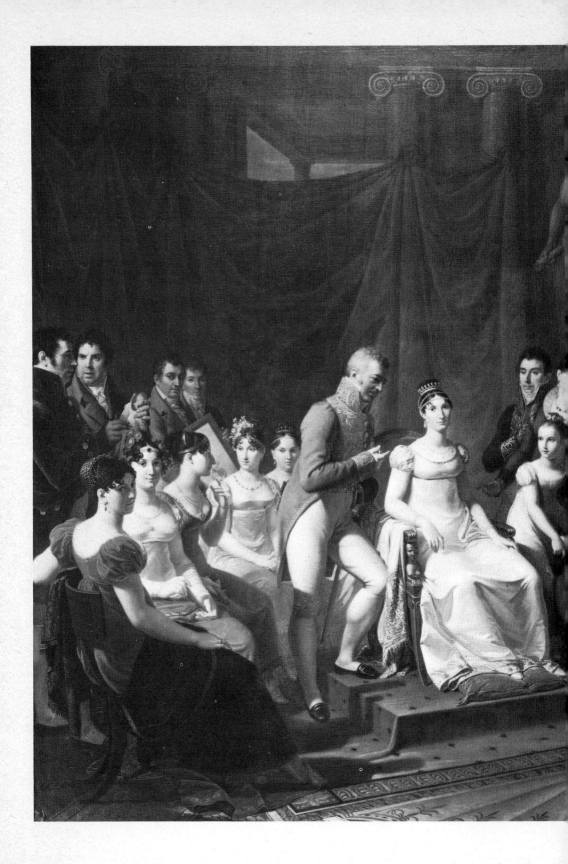

Bohemia, under the protection of the Austrian Emperor. The fact that Louis and his short reign are remembered with respect in Holland is an indication of his failure to fulfil his brother's demands and his determination to be 'King of the Dutch'.

Jérôme as King of Westphalia is remembered chiefly for his extravagance, luxury and sexual licence. It must be remembered, of course, that Jérôme, as the youngest, had no experience of the hardships of the early period of the family, and felt himself to be 'born to the purple'. His reputation for luxury has obscured the solid administrative achievements of the regime. No doubt this was largely due to the three efficient French bureaucrats with whom he was provided, Simeon, Beugnot and Jollivet. But Jérôme himself was an effective executive, when he was not being a play-boy, and a good judge of men. His prefects were all German, and efficient. Napoleon intended that Westphalia should be the model enlightened state of the new Confederation of the Rhine in contrast with the antiquated states of Germany. He wrote to Jérôme that 'It is necessary that your peoples should enjoy a liberty, an equality and a well-being unknown to the peoples of Germany.' The Napoleonic Codes were quickly and thoroughly applied.

Under the Constitution of November 1807, Westphalia was obliged to keep up an army of twenty-five thousand and in addition to support 12,500 French troops. In the year 1812, thirty-eight thousand were serving – a higher proportion than in any of the other satellite kingdoms. At first the budget was balanced, but the strain of the army and the support of French troops ruined the finances of the later years. Some 200 million francs went on the French troops.

In the crisis of 1809 there was a certain amount of guerrilla activity in north Germany, mainly attacking Westphalia. There was a conspiracy led by Dornberg, a colonel of Jérôme's guard, who raised some five thousand men to attack Cassel; they were defeated and scattered by Jérôme's Westphalians. The Prussian Major Schill's partisans entered Westphalia, were chased into Stralsund in Swedish Pomerania by Westphalian troops, and Schill was killed in the capture of Stralsund. In spite of the fact that Napoleon condemned Jérôme for his luxury on campaign and said that he 'made war like a satrap', he had in fact shown up well in successive crises. Less than a hundred of his own troops defected in 1809.

OPPOSITE Louis Bonaparte: a portrait by Jalabert. Louis's naturally paranoid temperament was aggravated by the effects of syphilis contracted in his youth. He treated Hortense with suspicion, believing rumours that she was having an incestuous relationship with Napoleon.

In January 1810 Westphalia acquired Hanover, but the quota of French troops to be supported went up to eighteen thousand. Meanwhile Napoleon had annexed northern Germany to the Empire in the interests of the Continental System, and the ruthless Davout was in charge. There were constant complaints about the Westphalian conduct of the system, and in October Jérôme wrote to Napoleon, 'If your Majesty's political designs require the re-union of the whole of Westphalia to the French empire, as its agents please themselves to put it about, I ask only that I should be the first and directly in the secret of these intentions.'

In 1811, as the Russian campaign approached, relations improved, and in 1812 Jérôme was given command of the right wing of the Grand Army. He thought it possible that he would be considered a candidate for the kingdom of Poland. Jérôme in 1811 was preoccupied with expanding his army, but in December 1811 he warned Napoleon of the growth of anti-French feeling: 'The powerful course of this dangerous movement is not only impatience with the yoke of the foreigner, but in the total ruin of the classes.' At St Helena Napoleon considered that:

I made a great mistake in making him King of Westphalia. I should have put there a minor German prince. Jérôme brought the luxury and wealth of the Crown of France into a poor place used to economy. In vain I told him to form a reliable Guard, a body of five or six thousand men on whom he could count, composed of the Corsican battalions and several French ones. He did not want it. He was afraid of not being sufficiently independent of the Emperor.

It was an evil day for King Joseph when he agreed with Napoleon to exchange the throne of Naples for that of Spain.

Throughout his dealings with Spain Napoleon's judgment showed at his worst. After Tilsit, it was noted that he was beginning to lose touch with reality, and to assume that all things must bend to his will. In his proclamation to the people of Madrid in 1808 he declared that 'God has given me the will and the force to overcome all obstacles.' From this attitude of mind sprang the catastrophic errors of the reign – the pursuit of the Continental System, the break with the Pope, the involvement in Spain and finally the breach with Russia.

Napoleon could see in Spain only the obvious fact so evident in the portraits of Goya that a decadent monarchy was holding back a people which, like Italy or the Rhineland, was waiting for

OPPOSITE Joseph Bonaparte, as King of Spain: by Kinson. A competent businessman, Joseph was nonetheless perhaps the least distinguished of the Bonapartes. He had married for money, and kept a number of mistresses.

enlightened reform and regeneration. He wrote that 'Spaniards are like other people and are not a class apart.' Spain was in effect ruled by Godoy, the lover of Queen Maria-Luisa, and her husband King Charles IV was a cypher. Godoy was opposed by Ferdinand, the Crown Prince, Prince of the Asturias, who was not much better.

In 1806, during the Jena campaign, Godoy had shown signs of disloyalty to the French alliance, since the capture of Buenos Aires by the British aroused fear that the whole of Spanish America might soon be lost. With the inauguration of the Continental blockade against Britain, Napoleon thought it necessary to control the whole of the Iberian coastline and peninsula. In July 1807 he began to concentrate troops for an invasion of Portugal and in October he obtained the secret treaty of Fontainebleau with Godoy by which Portugal was to be partitioned – the south as a principality for Godoy, Lisbon for France and the north for the Queen of Etruria in exchange for Tuscany, destined for Lucien or Elisa.

Meanwhile Ferdinand was also seeking Napoleon's support against Godoy. Two alternative lines of policy were thus taking shape in Napoleon's mind. He could either back Ferdinand and marry him to a Bonaparte princess, or he could sweep away the royal family by exploiting the dissensions between them. When he met Lucien in Mantua in December 1807, he was thinking of the first solution, when he asked that Charlotte, Lucien's daughter, should visit Paris. The unfortunate failure of the attempts at reconciliation with Lucien and his family led to the collapse of this policy, and events seemed to be leading automatically to the second solution. As Murat, appointed 'Lieutenant of the Emperor in Spain', was nearing Madrid, riots led to the fall of Godoy and the abdication of Charles IV.

Napoleon summoned the royal family to meet him at Bayonne, and wrote to Joseph to offer him the throne of Spain. Joseph refused, and Napoleon then turned to Louis, who also refused. Napoleon wrote to Louis:

The King of Spain has just abdicated: the Prince of Peace [Godoy] has been put in prison. An attempt at insurrection has broken out at Madrid. In this situation my troops were forty leagues away from Madrid. The Grand Duke of Berg should have reached it by the 23rd with forty thousand men. Up to this moment, the people call on me with urgent cries. Convinced I shall have no solid peace with England

OPPOSITE Julie Clary, wife of Joseph, with one of her daughters: by Lefèvre. Though devoted to her children, she found Joseph irritating and for her part had discreet affairs.

but by giving a big change to the Continent, I have resolved to place a French prince on the throne of Spain. The climate of Holland does not suit you. Moreover Holland cannot recover from its ruin. In this tempestuous world, whether there is peace or not, there is no means of maintaining it. In this situation, I think of you for the throne of Spain. Give me a definite reply. If I nominate you as King of Spain will you accept? Can I count on you? As it is possible that your courier will find me at Paris, and he may have to cross Spain in the midst of chances one cannot foresee, reply to me simply in these words, 'I have received your letter of such a date, I reply Yes,' and then I shall assume that you will do what I wish; or alternatively 'No', which means that you do not accept my proposal.

Napoleon then appealed to Joseph, and offered him Spain without conditions and without any cession of territory. This he accepted.

The result of the meeting at Bayonne was that Charles IV and Ferdinand both abdicated, in favour of luxurious exile in France. Napoleon assumed that any popular movements of protest in Spain could be dealt with by a short, sharp repression, as had happened in Egypt and in Italy. Even the rising in Madrid of 2 May did not disturb him. While Napoleon and Joseph were elaborating a liberal constitution for Spain at Bayonne, the provinces were flaming into spontaneous revolt. In the summer of 1808 Napoleon was faced with two severe blows to his prestige. Junot was forced to sign the Convention of Cintra and evacuate Portugal after the battle of Vimiero. Dupont, with two French divisions, was surrounded and forced to surrender by a Spanish army under Castanos at Baylen in Andalusia. When Joseph reached a silent and hostile Madrid, he was able to remain there for only eleven days before retreating hastily towards the Pyrennees. At Vittoria he met the Marquesa de Montehermoso who became *maîtresse en titre* throughout the Spanish period.

Joseph tried to tell Napoleon that the whole Spanish nation was exasperated and that he would prefer to return to Naples. But Napoleon refused to recognize that he was faced with a national resistance because the Spanish armies in the field could easily be defeated; and never until 1814 could he face the loss of prestige in removing his brother and replacing Ferdinand. There was also the lure of catching and defeating the English army in the Peninsula. On his side, Joseph never had the strength of mind finally to abdicate in face of his brother's wrath. There were always a considerable number of *afrancesados* among the official and urban classes who looked to Joseph for enlightened liberal reform. Joseph clung to the illusion that if he were left alone to give liberal government to the Spanish people, they would rally to his side.

In 1809 Joseph wrote to Napoleon:

It is a fixed truth that I cannot do any good without your absolute and exclusive confidence in the affairs of Spain. It is you who have given me this crown: if you find a man worthier than me of your confidence, let this man be king; as for me I shall always be what my conscience dictates, your brother and best friend, your most sure ally, a good Frenchman on the throne of Spain, because I am convinced that what is best for Spain and for France is their close union, their intimate alliance, but not the subjugation of one to the other. A subject Spain will be an enemy at the first opportunity. A Spain as a friend and sister will be always as is its king and your brother. I wish to obtain Spain for France and France for Spain; but, for that, it is necessary to persuade the weaker that the stronger does not intend to make it a slave. This opinion is the only enemy we have to deal with: the arms of the Spaniards would fall from their hands, they would all be at my feet if they knew what is in my heart. All would be the best friends of the French if they knew that, though I am a French prince, I wish what is my duty, and my duty is to govern them as a free and independent nation. If they saw that the promises contained in the constitution of Bayonne were to be realized, that nothing else is intended, then my thoughts are the same as my words, that every day I console myself for the disasters which afflict the country by the hope of seeing it happier eventually. I know well that the greatest happiness of a great people is independence as the greatest happiness of a man is a good conscience. I am now in the second stage of my life and will not change my principles at my age. If you do not think as I do, my precarious crown is at your disposition. Providence removed me from Naples, you may take back the crown of Spain.

Unfortunately the middle class was a small minority in Spain, and neither Joseph nor Napoleon could grasp the fact that the Spanish peasantry were attached to their monks, their nobles and their dynasty and would not accept reforms emanating from the French Revolution. They had even resisted reform when it was given to them by the enlightened Bourbon King Charles III in the eighteenth century.

After the meeting at Erfurt with the Tsar, Napoleon moved into Spain with the cream of the Grand Army, and brushing aside the Spanish troops, entered Madrid. Again in December 1808 Joseph asked leave to abdicate: 'I supplicate your Majesty to

A contemporary allegorical cartoon representing Spanish patriotism striking Joseph to the earth, his mask of hypocrisy at his side. The memory of Ferdinand VII is supported by an angel, and a lion, symbol of Castilian strength, grasps the sinister French eagle. In the background, a fortification represents Spanish resistance.

receive my renunciation of all rights he has given me to the throne of Spain. I prefer honour and probity to power bought so dearly.' At Madrid, Napoleon heard of Moore's presence in northern Spain, moved rapidly to catch him, and narrowly missed. In January 1809 he returned hastily to Paris to deal with the Austrian threat, and the plot concocted by Talleyrand, Caroline and Murat.

The British Government's decision to send Wellesley back to Portugal in 1809 was the crucial turning-point of the Peninsula War. The Spanish armies were everywhere defeated, and the guerrillas were beginning to flag. For Joseph the prospect looked brighter, and he was well received in Andalusia in January 1810. But Napoleon was annoyed at the failure of the French armies to combine and defeat Wellesley at Talavera, and after Wagram he intended to return to Spain himself. Also he could no longer tolerate the expense of Spain, which had already cost 300 million francs. In February 1810 he decreed that Catalonia, Aragon, Biscay and Navarre were to be 'military governments' under generals responsible only to Paris. This was total humiliation for Joseph, and contrary to his aspiration to be a 'Spanish' king. He was, in effect, left in control of only the centre of Spain, New Castile, as Soult was acting independently in Andalusia. Probably Napoleon intended to provoke him into abdication, but he would not contemplate the dismemberment of Spain and the desertion of his Spanish supporters. Napoleon, after the Austrian marriage, would not come to Spain himself, and sent Masséna instead who was defeated by Wellington's lines of Torres Vedras. In May 1811 Joseph visited Paris for the baptism of the King of Rome, and Napoleon agreed to subsidize him with a million francs a month, and to restore him soon to command of the armies in Spain. This was indeed implemented in March 1812, as Napoleon was preparing for the Russian campaign, and he could not trust overall command in Spain to one of the quarrelsome Marshals. In March 1812 Joseph had written to Napoleon:

Events have deceived my hopes. I have no longer any hope of being of any service. I pray Your Majesty then to permit me to place in your hands my right to the throne of Spain, which you deigned to transmit to me four years ago. In accepting this crown I had no object in view but the welfare of this vast monarchy. It has not been in my power to accomplish it. I pray your Majesty to receive me as one of your subjects and to believe that you will not have a more faithful servant than the friend whom Nature gave you.

In the spring of 1812 Wellington captured Ciudad Rodrigo and Badajoz, and in July he soundly defeated Marmont at Salamanca. Joseph had advanced to support Marmont, but not in time, and he had to evacuate Madrid and retire to Valencia. Wellington was unable to stay in Madrid, and had to retreat to Portugal from Burgos, but he now felt confident that the campaign of 1813 would be decisive. Napoleon had withdrawn many of the best French units for Germany, and Wellington was now reinforced to seventy-five thousand men, and had at last been appointed by the Cortes of Cadiz as commander-in-chief of all the Spanish armies. In January 1813 Napoleon advised Joseph that he should take up his headquarters at Valladolid to defend the north of Spain and the Pyrenees. He was late in abandoning Madrid, was constantly out-flanked by Wellington, and finally routed at Vittoria in June 1813. The French were not inferior in numbers or equipment and under an effective commander might have won, or at least avoided defeat. The news of the British victory played no small part in swaying Austria over to the side of the allies. Joseph retired in disgrace to Mortefontaine, and Soult was sent to defend the Pyrenees. In January 1814 Napoleon tried to negotiate with Ferdinand for his return to Spain, and in the end had to acquiesce in his return without conditions.

Joseph had been given an impossible task in Spain, but his illusions and ineffectiveness as an executive and commander were a contributory factor in the débâcle of the Spanish affair. Napoleon at St Helena summed up Joseph's faults:

The Spanish affair was not feasible with Joseph. Knowing him I should have realized this. He was the most incapable and precisely the opposite of the man required, because he did not do things himself and would not let others do them. This is what Bessières explained well. He went to the King to ask for orders. The King was ill or shut up with his mistresses. But the will to give orders and to work only seized Joseph once a month, and the army needed orders every day about food, pay, marching. He could not work with any general. He wished to com- mand but did not know how to, and could not. He let the troops die of hunger and I was obliged to extend the authority of the generals on the administration.

Of all the satellite rulers, Murat was the most troublesome, the most unpredictable and finally the most treacherous. Napoleon once said, 'He is king only because of her, of my sister.' This was a fact that Murat would never admit; he claimed to rule because of

The scene of battle at
Borodino, September 1811:
a contemporary artist's
impression. This French
victory was won at too high a
cost: forty-three French
generals had been killed or
wounded, not to mention the
thousands of rank and file.
Napoleon himself was
overcome with fever.

his own merit, his achievements and his contribution to the making of Napoleon, of which he did not hesitate to remind him. He was sensitive to opinion that he was a nonentity in the hands of his wife, like Bacciochi. Even as Grand Duke of Berg, Murat had started to rebel against the Emperor's orders. 'What! the Emperor asks me to be a sovereign in order to obey, to receive orders. There is a strange contradiction here.'

Caroline was not content to be a pretty woman, and a mother; she was a compulsive intriguer, obsessed, like her brother, with the lure of power. Nothing would ever satisfy her. No sooner had the Murats received the Grand Duchy of Berg than Caroline took advantage of Napoleon's absence in England in the winter of 1806 to seduce Junot. She chose Junot simply because, as Governor of Paris, he would be in a key position if the news arrived of Napoleon's death. Metternich, who became her lover in 1808, said of her, 'the head of Cromwell on a pretty woman'. Queen Hortense wrote of her in her Memoirs, 'Proud, determined, courageous, passionate, sensitive, the same charm which enslaved one to her did not conceal her ambition for complete authority and envy of all success.'

As the efficient lieutenant of the Emperor in Spain, Murat considered that he had the best claim to its vacant throne; and when he was informed that Joseph was to have Spain, and he, Murat, could have either Portugal or Naples, he fell ill with disappointment and chagrin. He had no hesitation in choosing Naples but, owing to illness, he did not set foot in it till September 1808.

Meanwhile Napoleon had driven a hard bargain. Murat was required to give up Berg and all his houses and possessions in France. Caroline was to succeed to the throne in Naples before her children if Murat died first. He had to pay the French troops of occupation, supply a contingent of twenty-one thousand men and enforce the Continental System. He found on arrival that Joseph had left the Treasury and the palaces empty, and had removed with him the most effective ministers, of whom only Saliceti remained. Murat was disappointed that he was not summoned to command the cavalry of the Grand Army in the 1809 campaign, but there was the danger of a British invasion. Murat acted with great energy in putting the administration to rights, capturing Capri from the British, forming a Neapolitan army of twenty thousand men and deterring the British invasion fleet. Murat and Caroline were popular with the Neapolitans because of the magnificence of their Court, Murat's exotic appearance and reputation and Caroline's beauty. But he was having trouble with Caroline, who was furious at being excluded from the Council of State, and intrigued with Ministers in her boudoir. Two parties formed at Court – Murat favoured a Neapolitan, even a pan-Italian, party, while Caroline resisted with the help of the French administrators and officers.

Murat protested against the Austrian marriage. Was not Marie-Louise the grand-daughter of Maria-Carolina of Naples, and might not Napoleon do a deal with her to restore her to the throne? In 1810 he was anxious to invade Sicily with the mixed force of forty thousand French and Neapolitans, and thought he had gained Napoleon's approval. In September 1810 he essayed a landing across the straits, but the French troops refused to move except on Napoleon's orders, which were lacking. Murat was furious at the sabotage of his operation, and complained to Caroline: 'He diminishes our revenues, crushes my trade . . . puts us in the impossible position of supporting this enormous burden with which he has saddled me. And when his policy or caprice make him decide to push me off the throne, it will be the same with me as with Louis.'

At the beginning of 1811 rumours were rife that Naples was to be merged into the kingdom of Italy. Napoleon told his Foreign Minister, Champagny, that 'The King deceives himself if he thinks that he can rule in Naples other than by my wish and for the general good of the Empire. If he does not change his system, I shall take possession of the kingdom and have it governed by a Viceroy like Italy. The King is not behaving properly. Whenever someone has repudiated the Continental blockade I have not spared even my own brothers. I shall spare him even less.' Murat's reaction was a rather childish assertion of Italian 'nationalist' moves. He built up his army, devised a new flag removing the tricolour and decided that all foreigners holding office were to become naturalized citizens of Naples. Napoleon retaliated by publicly humiliating Murat in a decree which made Frenchmen automatically citizens of Naples.

Murat fell ill with worry and frustration, and wrote to Napoleon in July 1811: 'If your Majesty only wishes to get rid of me, do not search for pretexts . . . a single word suffices and the King of Naples will cease to be an obstacle. . . . I never thought to be treated so barbarously.' Murat sent Caroline to Paris to smooth

things over, and she reported a long conversation with Napoleon on 16 November which concluded: 'Let him govern as he pleases, I shall leave him independent as long as his country enters in every way into the political system and interests of France.' As war with Russia drew nearer, Napoleon had need of Murat's services, and in May 1812 he was delighted to be told that he was to have command of the cavalry of the Grand Army. Caroline was appointed Regent of Naples in his absence. In retrospect Napoleon thought that 'It required at Naples a Viceroy and not a King. First of all a Viceroy who knew that his authority was precarious would not have constantly worried me. He would have been like Eugène'.

Thus it is apparent that the satellite rulers were in serious danger in the years 1809 and 1810. The birth of an heir to Napoleon and the title given him of 'King of Rome' portended an entirely new conception and reorganization of the Grand Empire. Not only had the federative system of vassal kings drawn from the Bonaparte family proved unsatisfactory, it was no longer necessary, and could be replaced by a unitary Empire with direct rule from Paris. Since 1803 Napoleon had been training and expanding his corps of civil servants, the *auditeurs* to the Council of State, of whom there were now three hundred. They were the future Prefects of the Empire. He boasted that 'With the help of my soldiers and my *auditeurs* I could conquer and rule the whole world.'

The fate of Louis therefore hung over the other brothers and Murat: they were temporarily spared by the preoccupations of the Russian invasion. But if this had succeeded, Napoleon would have resumed his plans for uniting the Empire, and discarding the vassal kings, whose pretensions annoyed him so greatly.

OPPOSITE Napoleon and the King of Rome: a drawing by Perigny. The child remembered his father with affection and loyalty.

7 The Débâcle of the Empire

When the Grand Army crossed the Niemen on 24 June 1812, Jérôme, Eugène and Murat represented the family. Jérôme did not last long. As the Russians persistently retreated and refused to give battle, Napoleon became irritated by the slowness of Jérôme's movements on the right wing. On 24 July, he wrote to Jérôme, 'You are compromising the success of the whole campaign on the right flank. It is impossible to wage war like this.' Shortly after, Berthier was instructed to send a message to Jérôme that 'The fruits of my manœuvres and the most magnificent chances in the war have been lost through his strange ignorance of the elementary principles of strategy.' At the same time Davout was authorized to assume command if Bagration's army could be brought to battle; but Napoleon omitted to tell Jérôme of this order. On 13 July Davout thought that he had at last caught Bagration, if Jérôme's third army could perform a pincer movement. He therefore notified Jérôme that he was assuming command.

Jérôme was affronted, sent a violent message to Napoleon refusing to serve under anybody but him and halted his troops. The following day he left his army to return to Westphalia with his body-guards. Davout was deprived of his chance of catching Bagration. Napoleon found Jérôme's conduct unforgiveable, but why did he put Jérôme, who lacked sufficient experience, in a key command?

Murat distinguished himself in the advance: Eugène especially in the retreat. While most of the Marshals were in favour of halting

An English cartoon illustrating the rise and fall of Napoleon.
Napoleon is depicted as a devil on the right, his chief adviser Talleyrand as a
devil on the left, and they are supporting a globe ravaged by the acts of
butchery by which the Emperor furthered his ambition.

the campaign at Vilna or Vitebsk, because of the high rate of wastage, Murat favoured advance. At the battle of Borodino he begged Napoleon for the Guard to complete a decisive victory, but Napoleon refused it. Murat's physical courage on the battle-field was much greater than his moral courage in adversity. When Napoleon left the army at Smorgoni after the passage of the Beresina, he had to designate a commander-in-chief. Murat's reputation with the troops and with the enemy was high. Berthier was unfit for independent command, Eugène was too junior as a commander, and Davout too unpopular with the other Marshals. He had to fall back on Murat, but in the circumstances it proved disastrous. He lost his nerve, and was unable to give any example or restore any discipline. He made no attempt to rest the army at Vilna or Kaunas and the remnants of the army disintegrated. Napoleon said to Caulaincourt, who accompanied him on his journey to Paris,

I fear Murat won't do anything necessary to reorganize the army. I should have done better to take him with me to Paris or to let him return to Naples. But he would not have come back for the reopening of the campaign and I should miss him with the young cavalry I shall have. He is attached to me but he has ridiculous ambition and vanity. He thinks he has superior political talents which he hasn't at all. The Queen has more energy in her little finger than the King in his whole body. They are jealous of Eugène because they covet Italy. The King wishes to persuade the Italians that that land won't have any existence or future unless the whole of Italy is united under the same sceptre. He hides his feelings from me, but is not so discreet with everyone else, these details come back to me. If the King outlasts me, he is capable of some folly but I shall settle that in advance. All the Frenchmen I have made kings have forgotten very soon they were born in *belle* France and that their best title is that of a French citizen.

On 11 December Murat wrote to Napoleon, 'Every human effort is hopeless to remedy the disorder. One can only resign one-self.' Yet Ney or Eugène could have done better. At Posen on 15 January, Murat handed over command to Eugène and set out for Naples, pleading ill-health. He refused to obey a letter from Napoleon, forbidding him to leave the army under any circum-stances. On 16 December, Berthier wrote to Napoleon that the 'King of Naples is the least capable man to act as commander-in-chief from any point of view. He should be replaced at once.'

In the *Moniteur* of 27 January, Napoleon published a reproof to

Murat. 'Because of ill-health, the King of Naples has given up command of the army which he has placed in the hands of the Viceroy. The latter is the more accustomed to the administration of important affairs; he has the Emperor's confidence.'

Eugène's Italian corps had been heavily in action at Borodino, and particularly distinguished itself in the drawn battle with Kutusov at Malojaroslavetz at the beginning of the retreat from Moscow. It was practically destroyed in the cold and hunger of the retreat. Eugène helped to save Ney when he, commanding the rearguard, had been cut off and given up for lost. His reputation, therefore, with the army as a whole was high. He conducted the retreat from Posen to the Elbe with skill and coolness, and was present at the first battle, Lutzen, of the 1813 campaign on 2 May. To his surprise and relief Napoleon gave him two months' leave from the Grand Army to supervise affairs in Milan, and to take command of the troops in Italy.

On his return to Naples in a bitter and discontented mood, Murat took the first step in betraying Napoleon and changing sides. Bernadotte had already shown such an example in 1812, but there was a difference. Bernadotte had ceased to be a French sub-ject on being elected Crown Prince of Sweden, and was not a member of the imperial family. Murat was a Prince of the Empire, and Grand Admiral of France. Murat found excuses to delay sending any Neapolitan troops northwards, and knowing that Austria, in the spring of 1813, was trying to act as mediator be-tween the allies and Napoleon, sent his aide-de-camp, Prince Cariati, to Vienna to sound out Metternich. At the same time he made approaches to Lord William Bentinck in Sicily. Metternich had been Caroline's lover in Paris in 1807, and he knew that in the end the decision would be hers. He guessed that Caroline had grasped, as he had, that Napoleon's ambition and obstinacy could end only in catastrophe, and that for the sake of her children's inheritance she would desert him.

In June 1813, after the inconclusive victories of Lutzen and Bautzen, Napoleon made an armistice. He needed a breathing-space to repair his losses and particularly to expand the cavalry. He needed Murat again to command the cavalry, and he suspected Murat of negotiating with the allies. He therefore summoned him to Dresden to justify himself. Murat and the Marshals begged Napoleon to accept the allied peace-terms offered by Metternich, but he refused.

OVERLEAF The devastation of Moscow by fire by its inhabitants in September 1812 which forced Napoleon's troops to retreat: an engraving after Notoff.

fini d'après Nature par Zotoff

Incendie de la Vi

VÜE DE LA VILLE DE MOSCOU,

en Septembre 1812.

Gravé par Gibèle en 1816.

DE LA DROITE DU KREMLIN.

He won his last major victory at Dresden, thanks largely to Murat's handling of the cavalry, but the final catastrophe came at Leipzig in October 1813.

Murat obtained leave from Napoleon to return to Naples but in the meantime Caroline, as Regent, had told Metternich's envoy that Naples would join the Allies. On 21 December, Murat wrote a last appeal to Napoleon to make peace: 'Make peace, make it at any price. If you refuse the prayers of your subjects, for your friends, you will destroy yourself, you will destroy us all.' On 8 January he agreed with the Austrian envoy a treaty of offensive and defensive alliance in return for the guarantee to him of the kingdom of Naples. Two days later he informed Napoleon of the treated and concluded, 'Because the ties of politics are momentarily broken between Your Majesty and myself, must those of friendship and family be broken too? I need to learn you are still my friend for I shall always be yours.' But his conscience was much troubled. He asked Julie Recamier, who was staying with the Murats, what he should do. She replied, 'You are a Frenchman, Sire, and you must be faithful to France.' 'Then I am a traitor,' he said, and covered his face with his hands. As for Napoleon, he wrote on 13 February, 'The conduct of the King of Naples is infamous, and the Queen's unspeakable.' Metternich stated in his Memoirs:

Caroline joined uncommon powers of mind to a pleasant exterior. She had carefully studied the character of her brother and did not deceive herself as to his defects or the danger to himself of his excessive ambition and love of power.... Her desire was to create for herself and her family a position as independent as possible of Napoleon and independent of the vagaries of his fortune – a fortune which she thought endangered by every act of violence resulting from his insatiable ambition.

Murat moved north with twenty thousand men to join the Austrians against Eugène, but he still refused to commit himself completely, and sent secret messages to Eugène that he would give him warning before attacking. The news of Napoleon's abdication in April arrived before hostilities could open.

An Austrian attempt to seduce Eugène from his loyalty to Napoleon met with short shrift. On 22 November 1813 the young Prince Thurn and Taxis was sent to Eugène by his father-in-law, the King of Bavaria, who had already changed sides, bearing letters from Austria offering Eugène the crown of Italy if he

145

would join the Allies. Without hesitation he gave his answer, 'It grieves me very much to have to say No to the King my father-in-law; but he demands the impossible.' 'It is not to be denied that the Emperor's star is beginning to wane, but it is only one additional reason why those who have received benefits from him should remain faithful to him.' Heavily outnumbered but not decisively defeated, Eugène slowly fell back to the line of the Adige.

As the shadows lengthened on the Empire, the Bonaparte family was gathering in Paris. Jérôme was expelled from Cassel by the advancing Russians, Louis arrived from Bohemia. *Madame Mère* was in Paris, but Pauline was wintering in the south of France. Elisa was still in Lucca, having allowed Murat's troops to occupy Tuscany, Lucien still in England. Elisa proclaimed that she had broken off relations with the French Empire, hoping to retain her possessions. In March 1814 a combined Anglo-Sicilian force landed at Leghorn, and marched on Lucca. Elisa and her husband Bacciochi were forced to flee to the south of France.

Louis wrote a conciliatory letter to Napoleon, suggesting that he should resume the throne of Holland, and help to keep the Dutch loyal to the Empire. 'I would rather return Holland to the Prince of Orange than send Louis back there,' was Napoleon's reaction, but he allowed Louis to return to France provided he came solely as a French prince.

Joseph, at Mortefontaine, was with difficulty persuaded by Napoleon to renounce his claim to Spain, though he insisted on retaining the title of King Joseph. Napoleon offered the crown to Ferdinand, but the Spanish Cortes refused to accept Ferdinand from the hands of Napoleon, and eventually he returned to Spain without conditions. As senior French prince and senior member of the family, Napoleon had no option but to give the post of Lieutenant-General of the Empire and Governor of Paris to Joseph, while he himself departed for the east for the campaign of France. The Empress remained Regent. It was a decision he was later to regret bitterly.

Outnumbered by four to one, his system of defensive warfare depended on threatening and attacking the flank and rear of the allied armies marching on Paris. This in turn depended on Paris acting as a fortified base, capable of holding out at any rate for a certain number of days. Before he left Paris in January, he gave orders to fortify Paris. If the Allies received information that

OPPOSITE *Madame Mère* in later years, wearing a high lace collar to conceal her wrinkled neck: painting by an unknown artist. She lived to be eighty-seven, outliving Napoleon, Pauline and Elisa, and enjoyed having Napoleonic memoirs read to her.

Paris would not hold out, his bluff would be called. Moreover he sent repeated orders that the Empress and the King of Rome must on no account be allowed to fall into the hands of the Allies. 'Get the Empress and the King of Rome to leave for Rambouillet; order the Senate, the Council of State, all the troops to gather on the Loire. I would prefer my son to be killed rather than see him brought up in Vienna as an Austrian prince.'

After initial defeats, which made the allies over-confident, Napoleon won successive victories in February over Blücher and Schwarzenberg at Champaubert, Montmirail and Montereau. But early in March he lost too many men in battles against Blücher at Laon and Craonne, and decided to retire eastwards and operate against the allied line of communications as they advanced on Paris. Meanwhile the allies received two vital pieces of information – a message from Talleyrand revealing the political war weariness of Paris and an intercepted message from Napoleon to Marie-Louise revealing his plan to turn east. Tsar Alexander persuaded the allies to march on Paris and ignore Napoleon. It was a political gamble, as he admitted afterwards that the allied army would have had to retreat if Paris had held out for another day. Marmont had barely twenty thousand men and some National Guards to cover Paris, which in fact capitulated in less than twenty-four hours. Napoleon arrived in Fontainebleau on 31 March, only to learn that Paris had capitulated a few hours before. Joseph had bungled the evacuation, because he persuaded the Empress, who was reluctant, to leave, but ignored Napoleon's instructions that the Government must also leave. He left Talleyrand and the Senate in Paris, free to treat as a Government with the Allies. On 1 April, a provisional government was formed, and two days later Talleyrand persuaded the Senate to decide the deposition of Napoleon.

There was still the possibility of a Regency for his son, and Napoleon had one asset, the loyalty of the army, who were bitterly opposed to the Bourbons. While Napoleon's Foreign Minister, Caulaincourt, was discussing a Regency with Tsar Alexander, news was brought in that Marmont had brought his corps over to the Allies. With this defection, and under pressure from the remaining Marshals, Napoleon wrote out his unconditional abdication. It was owing to the generosity of Alexander, not of Talleyrand or the Bourbons, that Napoleon was given Elba as a place of retirement. By the Treaty of Fontainebleau signed between Napoleon and the Allies, Napoleon was guaranteed the title of

OPPOSITE Louis, Joseph and Jérôme leave for Switzerland: a caricature published during the first restoration of the Bourbon monarchy. Joseph eventually settled in America.

148

Ils ont Chaud . . .
ou le Voyage en Suisse.

Napoleon abdicates at the
Palace of Fontainebleau,
20 April 1814: a
contemporary representation.

Emperor, the sovereignty of Elba, with a revenue of two millions
to be paid from the French funds, Parma for the Empress Marie-
Louise, and ample pensions for the members of the Bonaparte
family. On his way down to Elba, Napoleon visited his sister
Pauline, who was surprised and angry to find him wearing an
Austrian uniform. She refused to kiss him until he changed.
Napoleon had been so rattled by rumours of royalist plots and
mobs to murder him that he had resorted to this stratagem.
Pauline and *Madame Mère* were later in the year to join him in Elba.

All through the summer, Napoleon entertained hopes that his
wife and son would join him. The evidence of Marie-Louise's

letters to Napoleon shows that at the time of the abdication she was still in love with him, and fully intended to join him. She wrote to him:

I am sending you a few lines by a Polish officer who has just brought me your note to Angerville; you will know by now that they have made me leave Orléans and that orders have been given to prevent me from joining you and even to resort to force, if necessary. Be on your guard, my darling, we are being duped, I am in deadly anxiety on your behalf but I shall take a firm line with my father. I shall tell him that I absolutely insist on joining you, and that I shall not let myself be talked into doing anything else.

But once her father, the Emperor Francis, and Metternich arrived and she came under their influence, she had not sufficient will-power to take her own line. Napoleon must have realized that he had lost her when he received a letter from the Emperor Francis at Fontainebleau: 'I have decided to propose that she should pass some months in the bosom of her family.' Metternich arranged that her aide-de-camp should be General Count Neipperg, and by September he had accomplished his mission, which was to seduce Marie-Louise. The memory of Napoleon quickly faded and as Duchess of Parma she bore several children to Neipperg. A further sadness awaited Napoleon at Elba; in June he heard that Josephine had died on 29 May of diphtheria, aged fifty-one.

While the peace Congress was assembling at Vienna, the Bourbons in France were paving the way for Napoleon's return from Elba by their mistakes. The white cockade was substituted for the tricolour, and Louis XVIII refused to accept the liberal constitution drawn up by Talleyrand and the Senate except as a 'Charter' freely granted by a monarch by divine right. The humiliations of this first Treaty of Paris, the reduction of territory to the frontiers of 1792, could not be avoided, but the unpopular taxes of 1813 and 1814 were maintained, and the army was reduced by two-thirds. The Napoleonic Marshals kept their command and their properties, but they and their wives were snubbed at Court by the returned *émigré* nobles. The debate over the Press had aroused fierce reaction. Pasquier said, 'France was inundated with satirical pamphlets which represented the men in power as bent upon recalling the days of ignorance and darkness. The success of these writings was great; and public opinion henceforth shared their fears and their angers.'

The demobilization of the army was mishandled. The Maison du Roi was revived, with lavish posts for *émigrés* who had never seen fighting, and the Imperial Guard were degraded to 'Grenadiers de France'. Twelve thousand Napoleonic officers were put on half-pay. Several of the garrison-commanders were ready to march on Paris and overthrow the Bourbons, and they were in touch with Fouché who had been excluded from the new government. The proposal to restore national lands not yet sold to their original owners aroused the fears of the middle-class and peasantry about the land settlement. Most marked of all, the Bourbon Government refused to pay the pensions guaranteed under the Treaty of Fontainebleau. This made it literally impossible for

Napoleon to remain at Elba, and he could keep going only by borrowing large sums from his mother and Pauline. On the initiative of Wellington, as ambassador to Louis XVIII, her house in Paris, the Hotel Charost, had been sold to the British Government. Thereby the British possess as their embassy in France the finest house in Paris with a great deal of Pauline's furniture and silver. Napoleon was well-informed of developments in France and Europe by Joseph, now in Switzerland, and other correspondents. There were rumours at Vienna that he was to be removed to the Azores, the West Indies or St Helena.

Nor did Murat feel easy on his throne, in view of the hostility shown to him at the Congress. Talleyrand had asserted the initiative of France by laying down the principle of legitimacy which would include the restoration of the Bourbons to Naples. Royalist agents asserted that Napoleon and Murat were already in touch. By February 1815, when Napoleon had made up his mind to return to France, this was certainly true. Napoleon's instructions

Napoleon arrives at the island of Elba and is received by officials on the quay: a contemporary painting. The ex-Emperor was given a twenty-one-gun salute.

OVERLEAF Napoleon's house on Elba, the Palazzina de Mulini: engraved by Schroeder. He furnished it with borrowings from Elisa's villa at Piombino and from Prince Borghese – the ship carrying the latter's possessions was blown off-course between Turin and Rome, and landed at Elba.

to Murat were to wait until he, Napoleon, had established himself in Paris and then move north to secure Italy against the Austrians. Wellington, on his way from Vienna to take command of the British army in the Low Countries, wrote to Castlereagh that 'If we do not destroy Murat, and that immediately, he will save Buonaparte.' Murat, on the contrary, envisaged for himself an independent role, and was intoxicated by the dream of Italian unity under his banner. Caroline felt that Napoleon's gamble was doomed to disaster, and that safety lay in sticking to the Austrian alliance. But she was unable to prevail. Caroline told the Austrian envoy that

Murat believes that the possible success of Napoleon might help to maintain him on the throne. You know my opinion in this respect. I have done more: I have advised the King that if Austria replies that she has decided to oppose the Emperor Napoleon that he should join her and follow her policy. The King ought to adhere to a Great Power which protects him. If he tries to fly with his own wings he is lost. I held to the French system in the past until the last extremity because I was persuaded that our interests demanded it. Events have obliged us to change our policy. I am convinced that our safety depends on our intimate union with Austria and I hold to that with heart and soul. The Emperor Francis has supported us loyally up to now and I am sure he will not abandon us if we merit it.

On 17 March, before Napoleon reached Paris, Murat left for Ancona, and moved his troops northwards through the Papal States. From his headquarters in Rimini he issued a stirring proclamation to all Italians: 'The hour has come for the accomplishment of the great destinies of Italy. Providence summons you to be an independent nation. . . . I summon all brave men to join me in the fight.' But it produced few volunteers. He advanced to the Po at Ferrara, but was immediately forced to retreat, as the Austrians were being reinforced, and his own troops were deserting. He was caught and decisively defeated at Tolentino on 3 May. Caroline and the children were taken on a British ship the *Tremendous* to Trieste; Murat himself escaped by ship to the south of France, which he reached on 23 May, hoping to be employed by Napoleon. He received a message of 'the Emperor's regret that the King attacked without any consultation or agreement' and 'that he had ruined France in 1814; in 1815 he has compromised her and ruined himself'. It was made clear that he would get no employment, and was left to kick his heels in the south of France.

Then he heard the news of Waterloo, and was forced to escape to Corsica as his life was in danger from the White Terror against the Bonapartists. In Corsica he recruited three hundred men for a desperate landing in Calabria to raise his supporters against Ferdinand. He was caught as he landed at Pizzo on 8 October, and summarily court-martialled and shot. Caroline remained in Austria under police supervision with the incognito of Countess of Lipona. At St Helena Napoleon said of Murat after news of his death:

Murat lacked intelligence, although he had some education. He had been brought up to be a priest. I was wrong to let him marry my sister Caroline, but it was not my wish. It was his marriage which was his downfall. Murat, Lannes and Ney were the three bravest men of the army. But the bravest are capable of anything, even of cowardice, for lack of moral courage.

When Napoleon left Elba for his fantastic march to Paris, his last parting was with his mother and Pauline. Letizia recounts in her Memoirs how Napoleon broke the news to her of his departure the night before, and asked her opinion. She replied, 'Go, my son, fulfil your destiny, you were not made to die on this island.' Pauline gave Napoleon her diamonds.

On 1 March 1815, Napoleon landed unmolested near Antibes. He had with him a thousand men, including a few mounted Polish lancers. He told them that 'He would be in Paris without firing a shot.' He deliberately avoided the road through royalist Provence, and took the mountain road through Grasse, Digne and Grenoble. He was welcomed by the peasants of Dauphiné, who were enraged by the *émigrés* and the priests, but the crucial place was Grenoble. There was a strong garrison with a royalist commander. Napoleon knew however that La Bedoyère, one of his former aides-de-camp, commanded one of the regiments. When he found an infantry regiment barring the road, he told his men to trail their muskets, and advancing alone in his famous grey overcoat, he opened it and shouted, 'Here I am. Kill your Emperor if you wish.' They broke ranks and crowded round him with shouts of '*Vive l'Empereur!*' At Grenoble the gunners refused to fire, and the whole garrison went over to Napoleon. The next important city was Lyons, which the Comte d'Artois had to leave because of the hostility of the troops. Ney had promised Louis XVIII to bring Napoleon back 'in an iron cage' but when he discovered the

The people of Grenoble rush to welcome Napoleon on his spectacular march to Paris in March 1815: a contemporary painting.

temper of the troops, he suddenly changed his mind and announced that 'The cause of the Bourbons is lost for ever.' He had received a message from Napoleon saying, 'I will receive you as I did on the morrow of the battle of the Moskowa.' Louis XVIII departed for Belgium.

One of the first to greet Napoleon when he arrived at the Tuileries was Hortense. She tells the story of how the ladies of the Court discovered that the *fleur-de-lys* had merely been tacked over the imperial bees in the carpets of the Tuileries, and they spent the morning removing them. Hortense had annoyed Napoleon by accepting from the Bourbons the title of Duchesse de St Leu, but

in the excitement of his arrival, all this was forgiven. All Napoleon's brothers returned to Paris in the Hundred Days except Louis. *Madame Mère* arrived by sea from Italy with Jérôme and Fesch. The sisters were all absent – Caroline and Elisa were prisoners of the Austrians, and Pauline was kept in Italy under house-arrest by the Austrians.

Jérôme was given command of a division and fought courageously at Waterloo. Most surprising was the reconciliation of Lucien. He was bored with England and, as soon as the Continent was reopened in 1814, had returned to his Italian estate, where the Pope conferred on him the title of Prince of Canino. The political

OPPOSITE Louis XVIII at his
desk: a portrait by Gérard.
At the time of the birth of the
King of Rome, Louis's
comment had been: 'If God
has damned the world, then a
Bonaparte will not lack a
successor, but if, on the
contrary, the Divine wrath
abates, all the brats on earth
cannot save the temple of
iniquity from destruction.'

atmosphere in France was now very different, and more congenial
to Lucien as a politician. Napoleon's autocracy could not be resumed, and he found himself forced to grant a liberal constitution,
in the form of an *Acte Additionel* to the constitution of the Empire,
which in fact copied the constitution granted to Louis XVIII.

Lucien was restored as a Prince of the Empire, and made a
member of the Chamber of Deputies. He suggested that Napoleon
should abdicate forthwith in favour of his son, in order to appease
Europe, but after Waterloo he advised Napoleon to repeat
Brumaire and dissolve the Chambers, who were demanding his
abdication. The Chambers were divided in opinion. Some inclined to bargaining with the Allies on the basis of an abdication
in favour of the King of Rome, to keep out the Bourbons. Others
favoured the Orleanist branch of the Bourbons, while others
backed Lucien's backs-to-the-wall defence of Paris. Others again
demanded a Republic. Lucien's oratory once more came into
play.

What! Shall we still have the weakness to believe the words of our
enemies? When victory was for the first time faithless, did they not
swear in the presence of God and man that they would respect our
independence and our laws. Let us not fall a second time into the snare
set for our trust and credulity. Their aim, in endeavouring to separate
the creation from the Emperor, is to disunite in order to vanquish us
and replunge France more easily into that degradation and slavery
from which his action has delivered us.

But Lafayette countered by reminding his colleagues of the immense sacrifices France had made to support Napoleon's ambition. Finally Lucien had to admit defeat and advised Napoleon to
abdicate. Napoleon preferred to abdicate and retired temporarily
to Malmaison in the company of Hortense and *Madame Mère*. 'My
political life is over and I proclaim my son Napoleon II, Emperor
of the French.' But Lucien could not persuade more than a few
Peers to vote for Napoleon II, and the Chambers set up a provisional government under Fouché, who arranged for the hand
over to Louis XVIII.

Napoleon could not linger at Malmaison because if he fell into
the hands of Blücher, it was likely that he would be shot out of
hand. He left for Rochefort where there were two frigates, and the
plan was to sail for the United States. He made his last farewells
not only to his mother and Hortense, and his closest friends, but
also to his two illegitimate sons and their mothers, Alexandre and

Marie Walewska and Léon and Eléonore Denuelle. The boy Léon resembled the King of Rome, and politely explained that his school was divided into royalist and Bonapartists, and that he belonged to the King's party. Two more of his former mistresses also came, Madame Duchâtel and Madame Pellapra. Joseph accompanied Napoleon to Rochefort, and offered to stay and impersonate his brother. An immediate decision to embark for the US might have succeeded, as Captain Maitland, commanding the *Bellerophon*, did not get orders to intercept until a week after Napoleon's arrival at Rochefort. Hesitation was fatal, but Napoleon was turning over in his mind the more dramatic alternative of seeking asylum in England. A furtive escape in disguise to America did not appeal to him. Soon there was no option as a Bourbon Prefect was coming to take control at Rochefort.

On 13 July he surrendered at discretion to Captain Maitland, signing a letter to the Prince Regent, 'I have finished my political career, and I come, like Themistocles, to sit at the hearth of the British people.' Although he was careful to make no promises or guarantees, Maitland encouraged Napoleon to think that, like Lucien, he would be allowed to remain in England. But he did not realize that this would be politically impossible. The favourable reception given to Napoleon by the fleet and favourable demonstrations at Plymouth confirmed the fears of the Cabinet. Liverpool wrote to Castlereagh, 'You know enough of the feelings of people in this country not to doubt he would become an object of curiosity immediately, and possibly of compassion, in the course of a few months.' Hence it was decided to send him to St Helena, and by a Convention ratified by the Allies in August 1815, Britain was made responsible for Napoleon's custody.

OPPOSITE, TOP Napoleon aboard the *Bellerophon*, which was to take him to St Helena: a sketch by one of the British lieutenants, A. M. Skene.

BOTTOM Two plates from Napoleon's home on St Helena.

8 The Family in Exile

Joseph escaped from Bordeaux on an American brig. He was well received in the USA, and bought the estate of Point Breeze in New Jersey. He was known as the Comte de Survilliers, a title associated with the Mortefontaine property. Hundreds of crates of pictures and furniture were shipped from Europe to embellish Point Breeze. Before the Hundred Days, Joseph had turned a lot of cash into diamonds which he buried in Switzerland. He also acquired a tract of land in upper New York State, which he called his 'wilderness'. There he entertained his American mistress, Annette Savage.

His elder daughter Zénaïde married Lucien's eldest son Charles-Lucien, who became a famous ornithologist. His younger daughter Charlotte married Napoleon-Louis, the elder son of Hortense. In 1832, however, Joseph felt constrained by the progress of Bonapartism to return to Europe where he settled down in London. With the death of Napoleon's son in 1832, he was now the official Pretender, but his policy was one of quietism, of waiting till the French people recalled a Bonaparte. He disapproved of Louis-Napoleon's adventures, and complained that he behaved 'as if his uncle and father were dead'. Shortly before his death in 1844, he was reunited with his wife, Julie, in Florence.

By a law of 1816, the Bonaparte family were banished from France, and lost all their property, income and civil rights in France. Until Napoleon's death in 1821, international security restrictions and harassment of the Bonaparte family continued. The family tended to congregate in two centres – Trieste and

The daughters of Joseph Bonaparte, Charlotte and Zénaïde: a portrait by David.

BONAPARTE HOUSE
The late residence of
JOSEPH NAPOLEON BONAPARTE EX KING OF SPAIN,

Bonaparte House, near Bordentown, New Jersey: a contemporary American engraving. Joseph lived here during his exile.

Rome. After the Hundred Days, the Austrians released Elisa's Italian property, and she bought a town and a country house in Trieste. She had previously been interned in Brunn in the Austrian empire. She was released on condition that she took the title of Comtesse de Compignano. Jérôme and Catherine, now given the title of Count and Countess of Montfort by the King of Württemberg, arrived in 1819, and their children Mathilde and Jérôme were born at Trieste. But Elisa was the first of the brothers and sisters to die. Aged forty-four, she died at Trieste in 1820, and when the news reached St Helena, Napoleon remarked, 'Since Elisa has been taken, I shall soon follow.' Caroline, regarded as the most dangerous of the Bonapartes, was kept in Austria under Metternich's supervision. She was allowed to buy the castle of Frohsdorf, but moved to Trieste in 1824. Letizia found it impossible to forgive Caroline her treachery to Napoleon in 1814: 'If you could not control him you should have opposed him, but what battles did you fight with him, what blood flowed? It was only over your dead body that your husband should have pierced your brother, your benefactor, your master.'

Caroline was the worst off financially of the family, as she had

166

taken little from Naples. General MacDonald became her master of the household and her lover, and it was rumoured that they were secretly married. Her two sons, Achille and Lucien, both left for the US to join their uncle Joseph. Laetitia, the eldest daughter, married the Marquis Pepoli of Bologna in 1823. The younger daughter Louise married Count Rasponi of Ravenna in 1825.

Caroline received a substantial legacy under her sister Pauline's will, and she succeeded eventually in 1838 in extracting from the French government a pension of 100,000 francs a year, as the sister of Napoleon.

Achille Murat, one of Caroline's sons: drawn by Ingres. He was an eccentric who married a grandniece of Washington, became friendly with Emerson and spent much time experimenting with diets. He also wrote two books about America.

Caroline hoped that Achille would marry Joseph's daughter, Charlotte, but he took whole-heartedly to the American way of life. He married Catherine Wills, a great-niece of George Washington, and bought an estate in Tallahassee, Florida. His brother Lucien was dissipated and ran up huge debts which Joseph was forced to pay. He married an heiress, Caroline Fraser, and ran through her fortune, and they were forced to open a village school. The fourth child, Anna Murat, was to become a prominent figure under the Second Empire as a great friend of the Empress Eugénie.

Lucien, Prince of Canino, had returned to Rome after the Hundred Days. *Madame Mère*, Cardinal Fesch and Pauline also settled there. Louis was in Rome at first, later in Florence. Eugène had attended the Congress of Vienna, where his friendship with the Tsar brought him the promise of a principality to replace Italy. After the Hundred Days, in which Eugène took no part, no more was heard of this promise. But he was made Duke of Leuchtenberg and Prince of Eichstatt by his father-in-law, the King of Bavaria, and settled down in Eichstatt. He was given a palace at Eichstatt, and in 1821 built a palace in Munich. He was fairly rich as he was able to retain his properties in Italy and France. He died of a stroke in 1824. His daughter Joséphine married Oscar, the son of Bernadotte and Désirée Clary, Crown Prince of Sweden. Her descendants include the present monarchs of Norway, Sweden, Belgium and Denmark, and the heirs apparent of Greece and Great Britain. One son married the Queen of Portugal, the second the Grand Duchess Marie of Russia, daughter of Tsar Nicholas I. Another daughter married Pedro, Emperor of Brazil.

Hortense lost her title and her lover Flahaut, who married an English heiress, and bought the miniature *château* of Arenenberg on the Bodensee, in Swiss territory. She spent her winters in Rome, and was obliged by a law-suit to give up her elder son to Louis.

After 1818 Napoleon abandoned all hopes of release from St Helena, and his health was deteriorating. *Madame Mère* and Joseph both offered to join him in his exile, but were not allowed to go. Bertrand, the Grand Master of the Household, had written to Fesch, requesting that a priest, a doctor and a cook should be sent out to St Helena. Unfortunately Fesch and *Madame Mère* had fallen under the influence of a bogus clairvoyante, Madame

Kleinmuller, who persuaded them that Napoleon was no longer at St Helena. They therefore took no trouble about selection and sent two ignorant Corsican priests, and an unqualified surgeon, Antommarchi. It was not till the priest, Buonavita, returned in 1821, having left St Helena in March, that Pauline was able to persuade her mother that she had been the victim of a fraud. By this time it was too late.

Joseph was involved in several plans for rescuing Napoleon. A man was arrested in London for testing a submarine for this purpose. A fast frigate was waiting to sail when the news arrived of

The *château* of Arenenberg in Switzerland, to which Hortense retired in 1816. The name is derived from Narrenberg – 'Fool's Hill'. Here the future Napoleon III spent part of his childhood.

Napoleon at St Helena: engraved by Janet after Martinet. Here the disillusioned ex-Emperor lost the will to live and succumbed to the cancer that many of the male Bonapartes developed.

Napoleon's death. A house was built at New Orleans for his use, and a fast vessel, the *Seraphime*, was being constructed at Charleston. If Napoleon heard of all these plans, he now rejected them. He concentrated his remaining energies on his hopes for his son, and paved the way for his restoration by fabricating the Napoleonic legend. It was his last and not the least successful of his campaigns. In his Will, and in the writings of O'Meara, published in 1822 as *A Voice from St Helena*, and in those of Las Cases, *Memorial de Ste Hélène* (1823), Napoleon reconciled his career with the new forces of liberalism and nationalism. 'I recommend my son never to forget that he is a born French prince, and never to become the instrument of the triumvirate which oppresses the peoples of Europe.' Of the Bourbons he said to O'Meara,

They want to introduce the old system of nobility into the army instead of allowing the sons of peasants and labourers to be eligible and be made generals, as they were in my time; they want to confine it entirely to the old nobility. . . . Such were all the race, and such they have returned, ignorant, vain and arrogant as they left it. They have learned nothing, they have forgotten nothing. . . . I know the French. Believe me that after six or ten years, the whole race will be massacred and thrown into the Seine. They are a curse to the nation. It is of such as them that the Bourbons want to make generals. I made most of mine from the dust. Whenever I found talent and courage, I rewarded it. My principle was, *la carrière ouverte aux talens* [the career open to talents], without asking whether there were any quarters of nobility to show. It is true that I sometimes promoted a few of the old nobility from a principle of policy and justice, but I never imposed great confidence in them. The mass of the people now see the revival of the feudal times; they see that soon it will be impossible for their progeny to rise in the army. Every time Frenchmen reflect with anguish that a family for so many years odious to France, has been forced upon them by a bridge of foreign bayonets.

He made an apology for his Spanish policy:

If the government I established had remained, it would have been the best thing that ever happened for Spain. I would have regenerated the Spaniards: I would have made them a great nation. Instead of a feeble, imbecile and superstitious race of Bourbons, I would have given them a new dynasty that would have no claim on the nation except by the good it would have rendered to it. For an hereditary race of asses they would have had a monarch with ability to revive the nation sunk under the yoke of superstition and ignorance. Perhaps it is better for France that I did not succeed, as Spain would have been a formidable rival. I would have destroyed superstition and abolished the inquisition and monasteries of those lazy *bestie di frati* [beasts of monks].

He explained to O'Meara the breakdown of the Peace of Amiens:

After the treaty of Amiens I would also have made a good peace with England. Whatever your ministers may say, I was always ready to conclude a peace upon terms equally advantageous to both. I proposed to form a commercial treaty by which, for a million of English manufactured or colonial produce taken by France, England should take the value of a million of French goods in return. This was thought a heinous crime by your ministers, who reprobated in the most violent manner my presumption in having made such a proposal. I would both have made and kept a fair peace, but your ministers always refused to make one on equal terms, and then wished to persuade the world that I was the violator of the treaty of Amiens.

In spite of all the libels, I have no fear whatever about my fame. Posterity will do me justice. The truth will be known and the good that I have done, with the faults I have committed, will be compared. Had I succeeded I should have died with the reputation of the greatest man that ever existed. As it is, although I have failed, I shall be considered as an extraordinary man: my elevation was unparalleled because unaccompanied by any crime. I have fought fifty pitched battles, almost all of which I have gained. I have framed and carried into effect a code of laws that will bear my name to the most distant posterity. From nothing I raised myself to be the most powerful monarch in the world. Europe was at my feet. My ambition was great, I admit, but it was of a cold nature and caused by events, and the opinion of great bodies. I have always been of the opinion that the sovereignty lay in the people. In fact the imperial government was a kind of republic.

I certainly wished to make France the most powerful nation in the world but no further. I did not aim at universal dominion. It was my intention to have made Italy as an independent nation.

He told Las Cases that:

... liberal opinions will rule the universe. They will become the faith, the religion, the morality of all nations; and in spite of all that may be advanced to the contrary, this memorable aim will be inseparably connected with my name; for after all it cannot be denied that I kindled the torch and consecrated the principle, and now persecution renders me the Messiah.

Peace, concluded at Moscow, would have fulfilled and wound up my hostile expeditions. It would have been, with respect to the grand cause, the term of casualties and the commencement of security. A new horizon, new undertakings, would have unfolded themselves adapted in every respect to the well-being and prosperity of all. The foundation of the European system would have been laid and my only remaining task would have been its organization. Satisfied on these grand points and everywhere at peace, I should have also had my congress and my holy alliance. These are plans which are stolen from me. In that assembly of sovereigns, we should have discussed our interest in a family way, and settled our accounts with the people, as a clerk does with his master.

The cause of the age was victorious, the revolution accomplished: the only point in question was to reconcile it with what had not been destroyed. But that task belonged to me; I had for a long time been making preparations for it, at the expense perhaps of my popularity. I became the arch of the old and new alliance, the natural mediator between the ancient and modern order of things. I maintained the principles and possessed the confidence of the one: I had identified myself with the other. I belonged to them both: I should have acted conscientiously in favour of each.

He wished to establish the same principles, the same system everywhere.

A European code: a court of European appeal, with full powers to redress all wrong decisions, as one's redress at home those of our tribunals. Money of the same value but with different coins the same weight, the same measures, the same laws, etc.

Europe would soon in that manner have really been but the same people, and every one who travelled would have everywhere found himself in one common country. . . . I would have associated my son with the empire: my dictatorship would have terminated, and his constitutional reign commenced.

At Amiens I sincerely thought the fate of France and Europe and my own destiny were permanently fixed: I hoped that war was at an end. However, the English Cabinet again kindled the flame. England is alone responsible for all the miseries by which Europe has since been assailed. For my part, I intended to have devoted myself wholly to the internal interests of France: and I am confident I should have wrought miracles. I should have lost nothing in the scale of glory and I should have gained much in the scale of happiness. I should then have achieved the moral conquest of Europe, which I was afterwards on the point of accomplishing by force of arms. Of how much glory was I thus deprived.

One of my great plans was the rejoining, the concentration of those same geographical nations which have been disunited and parcelled out by revolution and policy. There are dispersed in Europe, upwards of thirty million of French, fifteen million of Spaniards, fifteen million of Italians, and thirty million of Germans; and it was my intention to incorporate these people each into one nation . . . with regard to the fifteen million of Italians, their concentration was already far advanced: it only wanted maturity. The people were daily becoming more firmly established in the unity of principles and legislation; and also in the unity of thought and feeling, that certain and infallible cement of human concentration. The union of Piedmont to France, and the junction of Parma, Tuscany and Rome, were in my mind only temporary measures, intended merely to guarantee and promote the national education of the Italians. The concentration of the Germans must have been effected more gradually: and therefore I had done no more than simplify their monstrous complication. Not that they were unprepared for concentration: on the contrary, they were too well prepared for it, and they might have blindly risen in reaction against us, before they had comprehended our designs.

At all events this concentration will be brought about, sooner or later by the very force of events. The impulse is given; and I think that since my fall, and the destruction of my system, no grand equilibrium can possibly be established in Europe, except by the concentration and confederation of the principal nations. The sovereign who in the first great conflict, shall sincerely embrace the cause of the people, will find himself at the head of all Europe, and may attempt whatever he pleases.

These sentiments had great appeal for the new generation which had not experienced the battlefields of the Empire, and laid the foundations of the Second Empire. In his Will, Napoleon left personal mementoes to the family, with the exception of Louis, but no money. His son, the King of Rome, got most of his personal belongings. Napoleon claimed to have deposited some six million francs with the banker Lafitte in 1815. By the time he died, there was actually $3\frac{1}{2}$ million available. Napoleon distributed legacies to his household at St Helena which amounted to 5,600,000 francs. In addition, he distributed his private domain which no longer existed. One half went to the officers and soldiers who had fought with him, the other half to towns which had suffered in the invasions of 1814 and 1815. In 1823 the personal legatees received a percentage of their legacies. Under the Second Empire a commission recommended that four million francs should be provided to complete the personal legacies, and another four million for the collective legacies. This went to surviving veterans, and the provinces and town affected by the invasions.

It was his grandfather, Emperor Francis, who took charge of

the infant King of Rome. Marie-Louise was at Parma, occupied with Neipperg and a new family; she rarely visited her son. He was to be brought up strictly as an Austrian prince, in the palace of Schönbrunn. The titles of King of Rome and Prince Imperial were dropped, and he became Duke of Reichstadt (of lands in Bavaria) and a Serene (but not Imperial) Highness. His French governess and attendants were dismissed, and his name was now 'Francis'. Dietrichstein, a fussy pedant, was appointed as his governor. He wrote:

It is necessary to banish everything that might remind him of the life he has led till now. People retain clear enough memories of their childhood years, that is to say of the age at which the Prince is now, to give

A drawing showing a project that had been put forward for a palace for the King of Rome in Paris on the Trocadero before Napoleon's fall.

us reason to fear, considering everything he is told, that he may one day hanker after the life he might have led. Above all, care must be taken not to instil into him exaggerated ideas about the qualities of a people to whom he can no longer belong, for fear that these ideas might follow him into the years of maturity. It seems to me that the Prince whose education I have been given the honour of directing must be considered as of Austrian descent and brought up in the German fashion. Many of the tendencies of his precocious sensibility must be gradually eradicated, without making him suffer and without hurting his pride more than is necessary.

His tutors were instructed to make him forget his father and everything French. As he had not seen his father since the age of

three this did not appear to be a difficult task. But he had inherited
some at least of his father's qualities, and one of the tutors des-
pairingly commented, 'He knows a great deal about the past, but
in this connection maintains a silence which is quite extraordinary
in a child.' He wept bitterly when the news was broken to him that
his father had died at St Helena. Metternich forbade the executors
of Napoleon's Will to come to Vienna to hand over the possessions bequeathed to his son. Dietrichstein explained that the
'Prince is not a prisoner . . . but he is in a very special position'.

As he grew to manhood he was able to read works like Las
Cases which fired his imagination. In 1828 he was given a cap-
taincy in a Tyrolean regiment, and in 1830 the colonelcy of a
battalion. Between 1830 and 1832 there were revolutionary up-
heavals in France, Belgium, Poland and Italy which seemed to
offer prospects and opportunities for the young prince. There
were manifestations in his favour in France.

In November 1830 Elisa's strong-minded and enthusiastic
daughter Napoleone came to Vienna, caught a glimpse of
Reichstadt and wrote to him:

In the name of the fearful torments to which the Kings of Europe
condemned your Father, the exile's agony by which they made him
expiate the crime of having treated them too generously, remember
that you are his son, that his dying gaze rested on your portrait, and
show your awareness of so great an honour, and inflict no other
punishment on them than that of seeing you seated on the throne of
France.

Reichstadt made no response to this gesture.

He also met Marmont at a ball in Vienna, and had many talks
with him. Marmont recalls that:

. . . his eyes, smaller than Napoleon's and deeper set, had the same ex-
pression, the same fire, the same energy. They were big blue eyes sharp
and piercing and perpetually on the move. His forehead too recalled
that of his father, and there was another point of resemblance in the
lower part of the face and chin. Finally his complexion was that of the
young Napoleon: the same pallor and the same colour of the skin.

In 1832 his friend Prokesch visited *Madame Mère* in Rome with
news of her grandson, 'You will tell him that above all he must
respect his father's wishes. His hour will come. He will ascend the
throne of France.' But their hopes were doomed. Not only had the
isolation in Vienna in which he had been brought up left him un-

179

known and mysterious, but he was already fatally ill with tuber-
culosis, the hereditary malady of the Habsburgs, which the
doctors failed to diagnose. In his last illness, he said, 'Between my
cradle and my tomb there is a great nought.' He died on 22 July.

Meanwhile the two sons of Louis and Hortense, Napoleon-
Louis and Louis-Napoleon had plunged into an active part in the
revolutionary movements in Italy. They joined the insurgents in
Bologna, and Louis-Napoleon wrote to his mother that 'The
name we bear obliges us to help a suffering people that calls upon
us.' Actually the insurgents were embarrassed by the two young
Bonapartes, as they were relying on help against Austria from
Louis-Philippe, and asked them to leave. Napoleon-Louis died of
measles at Ancona in their flight, and Louis-Napoleon was seriously ill with it. He was rescued by his mother, who smuggled
him out of Italy, and got to Paris.

These two deaths, so near to each other, drastically altered the
family succession. Joseph was now again the titular head of the
family, and the official Pretender. After him now came the twenty-
four-year-old Louis-Napoleon. Brought up and spoiled by his
mother, he was a dreamy, romantic, indolent small boy. His tutor
Le Bas, who was the son of a notorious Jacobin, was appointed in
1819 and reported that he was backward, ignorant, lazy and with a
dislike for working; he might be a seven-year-old rather than a
twelve-year-old. Le Bas put him through a rigorous discipline and
time-table of $9\frac{1}{2}$ hours' work a day. In the six years of his tutor-
ship, he transformed him into an independent and athletic young
man, with habits of study which he maintained in subsequent
years and during the six years of his imprisonment.

Joseph wanted a quiet life, and would take no active steps to
promote the Bonapartist claims. Louis-Napoleon was ardent,
romantic and eager for action. He wrote at this time, 'I have
chosen as my principle of life to go forward always in a straight
line . . . hoisting myself high enough so that the dying rays of St
Helena may still clear my way.' Back at Arenenberg, he could only
write pamphlets – *Rêveries Politiques, Considérations Politiques et
Militaires sur la Suisse, Manuel d'Artillerie*, which at least made his
name known. In the *Rêveries Politiques* he discussed the regeneration of France: 'My own belief is that it can only be done by com-
bining those two popular causes, Napoleon and the Republic.' In
1835 he met Persigny and they planned the *coup d'état* of Strasbourg. It was chosen because it was a frontier town, radical and

republican in feeling, but had also enjoyed great prosperity under the Empire. In 1832 there had been a plot in Strasbourg to proclaim Napoleon II. Louis-Napoleon's one asset was the adherence of Colonel Vaudrey, commander of one of the artillery regiments and a veteran of Waterloo. But the other regiments were not won over, and the conspirators were soon rounded up and put under arrest. Louis-Napoleon's attempt in 1836 to raise the garrison and town of Strasbourg was a farcical failure, but Louis-Philippe wisely refused to make a martyr of the young prince, and shipped him off to America without a trial.

He had to return because he received word that his mother was dying. The elder generation of Bonapartes was now beginning to disappear. Pauline had died in 1825, aged forty-four. *Madame Mère* died in 1836, aged eighty-six. Caroline died in 1839, aged fifty-seven; Lucien in 1840, aged sixty-five; Louis in 1846, aged sixty-eight. Of all the brothers and sisters, only Jérôme survived into the age of the Second Empire.

The French government now made a mistake by threatening Switzerland with war if she did not expel Louis-Napoleon. This diplomatic incident only helped to make his name known to the whole of Europe and improved his image as the persecuted prince. He retired to London, and in 1839 published his most substantial pamphlet, *Des Idées Napoléoniennes*, a distillation of the legend which he had inherited from St Helena. 'The Napoleonic Idea consists in a reconstitution of French society overturned by fifty years of revolution, and a reconciliation of order and liberty, the rights of the people and the principles of authority. Napoleon's wars were forced on him by the Allies: if sometimes he seemed to be the aggressor, it was because he wished for the advantage of the initiative. The aim of all his wars and conquests was a Holy Alliance of Europe – a solid European association, based on the sovereign rights of each nationality and the satisfaction of their common interests.' It sold well, and went into four editions.

Events in 1840 seemed to favour Bonapartism. France's championship of Mehemet Ali in the Near East had led to a revival of the Waterloo coalition against France, and there was a good deal of chauvinism in the army. Louis Philippe attempted to exploit Bonapartism and render it harmless by bringing back the body of Napoleon from St Helena, and burying it in the Invalides. To Louis-Napoleon it seemed a crucial moment for another attempt at a military *putsch*. He hired a paddle steamer, the *Edinburgh Castle*, and sailed to Boulogne with fifty-six men, banners, proclamations and a tame vulture in a cage. In his proclamation to the French people he said: 'The ashes of the Emperor shall not return except to a France regenerated. . . . Glory and liberty must stand by the side of Napoleon's coffin. I feel behind me the Emperor's shadow urging me on: and I shall not halt until I have recovered the sword of Austerlitz, replaced the eagle on our banners and restored the people to its rights.' The attempt was even more of a fiasco than that of Strasbourg. He had the second-in-command of the detachment of the 42nd Infantry Regiment at Boulogne on his side, but not the commanding officer, who acted promptly and firmly by turning out Louis's supporters from the barrack square and shutting the gates against them. After planting his tricolour at the Colonne de la Grande Armée, commemorating Napoleon's attempt to invade England in 1805, Louis-Napoleon was captured as he was reaching a boat off-shore. All his followers were captured with the exception of two who were killed.

But this time the French Government could not brush it off without a trial. Louis-Napoleon was tried by the Court of Peers, and condemned to perpetual imprisonment in a French fortress. He used the trial with great effectiveness for propaganda, challenging the whole basis of the Orléanist regime. As he was taken to the fortress of Ham, on the Belgian border, it seemed that Bonapartism was finished. But as Louis-Napoleon murmured, 'How long is perpetuity in France?' It turned out to be six years. In the meantime, he continued to study and to publish articles and pamphlets. The most important was *L'Extinction du Pauperisme*, in which he tackled the social question, and incorporated into Bonapartism the Saint-Simonian and Socialist ideas which were penetrating the working-class in the 1840s. He refused offers of pardon, on condition that he renounced all claims to the French throne.

In 1846 he escaped from the fortress to Brussels and London by the simple process of disguising himself as one of the workmen repairing the buildings.

In 1848 came his big opportunity. Louis-Philippe was overthrown in the February Revolution, and the Republic was proclaimed. By this time Louis-Napoleon had learned the value of patience, and was determined not to force events. He appeared in Paris on 28 February but withdrew at the request of the Assembly, leaving Persigny and Prince Napoleon in Paris to organize a Bonapartist movement. Louis-Napoleon wrote of Prince Jérôme,

Candidat présenté par Nicolas, appuyé par la Presse.

MAIS NON, PUISQUE C'EST LE CHAPEAU DE L'EMP'REUR.

HA ÇA !.... MAIS.... MAIS C'EST UN ÂNE!

What at bottom I find at fault in him is his incalculability. There are people one understands and knows at a first meeting. Whether you like them or dislike them, you know at once the kind of person you are dealing with. But Prince Napoleon is sometimes frank, loyal and honest, sometimes stiff and underhand. At one moment he shares in heart to heart talk about your ambitions . . . at another moment his conversation is dry, scabrous and futile. What am I to believe? I always hope for the best, so long as I have no proof of the opposite; and while I am always on my guard, I put no curb on my impulses of kindness and friendship.

The relationship between the cousins throughout the Second Empire was to be chequered and stormy. It was noticeable that in the April elections of the new Assembly, his cousin Prince Napoleon, son of Jérôme, Prince Pierre Bonaparte (son of Lucien) and Prince Lucien Murat were elected. In the supplementary elections of June, Louis-Napoleon was elected for Paris and three other departments. He resigned in deference to the conservative Assembly; but at the same time the decrees of banishment were repealed.

Events were playing into his hands. The Assembly provoked a confrontation with the Paris workers by cancelling the dole for the unemployed, and the June workers' rising was bloodily suppressed. The Republic was doomed from this moment, though it lingered four years. In September Louis-Napoleon was elected for five separate Departments and this time quietly took his seat. In November the constitution of the Republic was voted, which provided for a President elected by universal suffrage. Louis-Napoleon received $5\frac{1}{2}$ million votes out of 7,300,000. His nearest rival, the Republican conservative Cavaignac received $1\frac{1}{2}$ million votes. This tremendous victory was largely the triumph of the name of his uncle and the legend, but it also owed something to Louis-Napoleon's active promotion of the Bonapartist cause. Not only the bourgeoisie, who wanted order and safety from the Red Peril, could vote for Louis-Napoleon but also the workers who hated Cavaignac and the Republic which had suppressed them in June. The monarchists could hope that Louis-Napoleon would be a stepping-stone for a restoration.

It was Louis-Napoleon's hard-won belief in patience that delayed the coming of the Second Empire for four years. In 1849, elections produced an Assembly more royalist and reactionary than its predecessor, but with a strong Left led by Ledru-Rollin.

The Left made an abortive insurrection, and the Right retaliated by a law in 1850 restricting universal suffrage. Louis-Napoleon cleverly exploited both events to discredit the Assembly. He stood as the champion of order against anarchy and at the same time as the champion of the plebiscite, the source of his authority, and of universal suffrage against a reactionary Assembly. Nobody believed that the Constitution could last. The expiry of the President's term would be the signal for a monarchist or Bonapartist or Republican *coup*. The Chambers could not agree on a revision of the Constitution. An Algerian general, St Arnaud, was appointed Minister of War. The principal planner of the *coup* was de Morny, Louis-Napoleon's illegitimate half-brother. Prince Jérôme was excluded because he was unreliable and disapproved. The Empress Eugénie said afterwards of de Morny that:

... he possessed in a high degree most of the qualities of real statesmanship; a sense of realities and possibilities, clearness of vision, readiness and subtlety of mind; he spoke temperately and to the point; stuck to his purpose, but with as little imperiousness as weakness; was cool, ingenious and secretive in action; he had the subtle art of leading and managing men. Moral considerations apart, Dec. 2nd, which was mainly his work, was a masterpiece. ... How far superior to Brumaire, when lack of foresight was only equalled by clumsiness, and Bonaparte himself lost his head.

De Morny warned that the dangerous period would be the third day. A few barricades began to go up, and the army overreacted, causing a massacre of some fifty citizens in the Boulevard des Italiens. In the provinces some twenty-seven thousand Republicans and Socialists were arrested. But the subsequent plebiscite gave $7\frac{1}{2}$ million votes for Louis-Napoleon, 650,000 against. The new Constitution returned to the Consulate of Napoleon I – a head of state elected for ten years, a Council of State, Senate and Legislative Assembly. The establishment of the Empire a year later required little fundamental constitutional change.

9 The Second Empire

Napoleon III, like his uncle, was not lucky in his relatives. The principal trial, though there were many others, was King Jérôme and his son Jérôme, who were the heirs presumptive until the birth of the Prince Imperial. King Jérôme had fought well at Waterloo, but he was dissipated and wildly extravagant, as always. After the death of his wife Catherine in 1835, he was more than usually impoverished, and married a rich Tuscan widow, the Marchesa Bartolino-Baldelli. The elder son had died in 1847, and the younger was known as 'Plon-Plon', a nickname which came from his childish attempts to pronounce the name Napoleon. He was quite as dissipated as his father, but meaner, and from his youth took up a republican and extreme democratic position. A bitter diarist of the Second Empire, Viel-Castel, described Plon-Plon as 'an appalling cad who plays the part in relation to the President that Philippe Égalité played in relation to Louis XVI'. In his youth, he was said to resemble the great Napoleon, and he had intelligence and vivacity. His faults were impetuosity, tactlessness and lack of application. After his mother's death, the family had spent several months with Hortense at Arenenberg, where Louis-Napoleon became fond of his young cousin, and fell in love with his sister Mathilde. There was an engagement, which was broken off after the Strasbourg attempt in 1836, which infuriated King Jérôme. He then encouraged his daughter to marry Prince Demidoff, an enormously rich Russian. The Demidoffs were ironmasters of humble origin, and Demidoff was dazzled by Mathilde's royal connections. He was however of bad and sadistic

Mathilde, one of the daughters of Jérôme and Catherine of Württemberg:
a portrait by Dubuffe. It had been said in her youth that she 'shone stunning
as a diamond'. Separated from Demidoff, she lived on his money with her
lover, the sculptor Nieuwerkerke, until the fall of the Empire.

character, already ill with syphilis. The Tsar took Mathilde's side, and granted her after a few years a separation from her husband, stipulating an allowance of 400,000 francs a year, of which she paid over 40,000 francs to her father. The Demidoff wealth enabled her to keep a salon and play the part of patroness of the arts in Paris, and she had fallen in love with a Dutch sculptor named Nieuwerkerke, who remained her lover for twenty-five years. As a special concession and exception to the law of exile, King Jérôme and his family were allowed to reside in Paris from 1847.

In 1847 Napoleon had written to Plon-Plon, 'It is very sad to think that neither you nor I have a child. There will be no more Bonapartes except the bad Lucien branch.' This was the position which made it desirable for Louis-Napoleon to keep on good terms with the Jérôme branch. He heaped favours on King Jérôme. In 1848 he was made Governor of the Invalides with a salary of 45,000 francs, in 1850 Marshal of France with 30,000 francs and in 1851 President of the Senate, with the Palais Royale as a residence. But he lost Mathilde's pension of 40,000 francs. With the proclamation of the Empire, his position improved dramatically. He received a million francs allowance from the Civil List and numerous residences with an allowance of three million francs to keep them up, and Plon-Plon received 200,000 francs. King Jérôme died in 1860, actually solvent for the first time.

In 1848, Louis-Napoleon had disposed of Plon-Plon for the time being by sending him as Ambassador to Madrid. But after a short stay, he had to be recalled for blatant intrigues with the opposition to the Spanish Government. He was not in the secret of the *coup d'état* of 1851 and disapproved of it. Louis-Napoleon received far more help from his illegitimate relations. His half-brother, the Comte de Morny, son of Flahaut, was the organizer of the *coup d'état*. Comte Walewski, son of Maria Walewska, was a competent Foreign Minister in the 1850s. Unfortunately the Comte Léon turned out to be a disreputable and dissipated blackguard and gambler: he was penniless at the beginning of the Second Empire, but Louis-Napoleon paid his debts and gave him a pension of 50,000 francs. He died in 1881.

During the period of the Crimean alliance with Britain, there was talk of Plon-Plon's marrying the Princess Mary of Cambridge, first cousin of Queen Victoria. This was favoured by Palmerston

Alexandre Walewski and his wife. Comte Walewski served loyally as ambassador to London and during the Second Empire was Minister of War. His illegitimate son Antoine followed his example and entered the French consular service.

but vetoed by Queen Victoria, on the ground of difference of religion. Naturally the marriage of Louis-Napoleon to Eugénie de Montijo came as a shock to Jérôme and Plon-Plon, and created a situation somewhat similar to the Beauharnais–Bonaparte feud in the First Empire. Plon-Plon remarked, 'One may make love to Mademoiselle de Montijo, but one does not marry her.'

Her father, the Count de Montijo, was a grandee of Spain and an *afrancesado*, a supporter of King Joseph. She had been brought up in a Bonapartist atmosphere. Her mother was Scots, the daughter of William Kirkpatrick, a wine-merchant. Eugénie's elder sister,

ABOVE The Empress Eugénie: a portrait after Winterhalter. This was the cool beauty with whom Napoleon fell 'so naïvely and so seriously' in love, and of him she wrote: 'He is capable of great sacrifices and small gestures.'

LEFT Napoleon III; a portrait by Flandrin. This nephew of the first Napoleon was to show his talent as a politician and was in tune with his age. However, he never overcame the over-indulgent side of his nature.

Paca, made a brilliant marriage to the Duke of Alba. Plon-Plon openly sulked when he was asked to sign the register as a witness to the birth of the Prince Imperial.

In the Crimean War, Plon-Plon was given command of the Third Division of the Army of the Orient, but muffed his chances of glory. He behaved well at the battle of the Alma, but could not stand the prospect of discomfort and boredom involved in the

Napoleon and Eugénie with their son, the Prince Imperial: a family photograph. The Prince was highly intelligent, particularly talented in drawing and sculpture, and doted on not only by his parents but by all around him.

decision to besiege Sebastopol. He threw up his command and returned to Paris, thereby incurring the charge of cowardice. Queen Victoria, on her visit to Paris, found him unlikeable: 'He seems to take pleasure in saying something disagreeable and biting, particularly to the Emperor, and with a smile that is quite satanic.' He was given another chance when he became Minister for Algeria in 1858. He was in favour of a forward policy in Italy, and it was Plon-Plon's own idea, not Louis-Napoleon's, to ask for the hand of Princess Clotilde, daughter of King Victor Emmanuel of Savoy. Cavour had no option but to favour it, for fear

Napoleon-Joseph ('Plon-Plon') and his wife Princess Clotilde, photographed at the International Exhibition in 1862. Behind them are a piece of Gobelin tapestry and other exhibits.

of offending France, if it was opposed. In the Italian War of 1859, Plon-Plon was given command of the Fifth Corps in Tuscany, but took no part in the battles of Magenta and Solferino. He was, however, an effective negotiator with Emperor Francis Joseph, in presenting the terms of the armistice of Villafranca. In 1860 he bought the estate of Prangins, which had originally been King Joseph's, in Switzerland, and built there a modern villa. With the death of the Duc de Morny in 1865, it looked as if the prospects of political responsibility for Plon-Plon were brighter. But again, as Vice-President of the Council, he made a tactless speech at Ajaccio, advocating measures of liberalization of the Empire going far beyond the official policy. He was publicly rebuked by Louis-Napoleon and retired into private life.

Thus he had nothing to do with the policy that led up to the Franco-Prussian War, and regarded it as folly. He predicted that 'This time it is the great departure, we shall never come back.'

When his small son once asked the Emperor what was the difference between an accident and a misfortune, Louis-Napoleon replied: 'If your cousin Plon-Plon falls into a well that is an accident: if he gets out, it is a misfortune.' Princess Mathilde blamed Eugénie for the catastrophe:

I shall prove what has come to be my profound conviction, that she was the principal cause of our misfortunes. She took eighteen years to destroy the Emperor, and she wore him out. This woman, who is called virtuous because she had no lovers, ruined the best and most generous of men and our poor country with him. She undermined our Society by her excessive luxury, by setting the example of boundless coquetry, by constantly giving more importance to the outward appearance of men and things than she did to their essential qualities.

Her niece Caroline Murat thought that 'It is possible, indeed very probable that had my aunt been Empress of the French the Franco-Prussian war would never have taken place. She would have made an admirable Empress.'

Apart from the major headache of Plon-Plon as the heir presumptive, Louis-Napoleon was plagued by the lesser members of the clan. First of all there was the embarrassing position of Betsy Patterson, Jérôme's American first wife. Betsy revisited Europe in 1815 and 1816 and returned in 1819 with her son, 'Bo'. They visited Rome in 1821 and 1822, and met Pauline and *Madame Mère*, who were much taken with the attractive son. *Madame Mère* wrote to Joseph, 'I am amazed at him. It is hardly possible to find so much aplomb and good sense in one of his age.' There was now a plan to marry him to Charlotte, Joseph's second daughter.

Betsy wrote home lively but malicious impressions of the family. Of Pauline she said, 'They say she is good *au fond*. I cannot say I have the least reliance on that family. They are less wealthy than is supposed. I believe some of them are amiable but when there is a question of parting with money, good will is generally exposed to a great trial.' 'The King of Westphalia spends everything he can get hold of and will keep up kingly state until his expended means leave him a beggar. Joseph is said to be the richest and is a man of sense.' Betsy thought that the only Bonaparte in Rome with any sense was 'the old lady'. 'She is very sensible and very miserly, and probably will leave all she can save to her children, who are all spendthrifts.' Bo was staunchly American, and though fond of the family, disliked their idleness and extravagance. 'I am glad I came to Rome to see my family,' he wrote to his grandfather, 'but their mode of living and thinking is so entirely different from my habits of living and thinking that I do not enjoy my residence in Rome.' They breakfasted between twelve and one, they dined between six and seven, they had tea at midnight.

Bo returned to America to see Joseph, but he vetoed the match, partly because Betsy Patterson demanded an enormous dowry. He visited his father in 1826 and 1827, but on his return to Baltimore married a local girl, Susan Mary Williams. His elder son, Jerome Napoleon Bonaparte Jr was born in 1840. Betsy's last visit to Europe was in 1839. Bo visited Paris in 1854, with the idea of obtaining a military commission for his son from Napoleon III. King Jérôme and Plon-Plon objected to Bo's living in France, and demanded that the Family Council should forbid him to use the name of Bonaparte. The Council decided that he was entitled to the name, but to nothing else. On the death of King Jérôme, the Pattersons in 1866 opened a formal law suit in Paris on the validity of Betsy's marriage. The Court decided that the Patterson marriage was null and void in France, but Bo's son, who had served in the French army in the Crimea, was allowed to keep the Bonaparte name, and received an annual pension of 30,000 francs from the Emperor. Betsy died in 1879 at the age of ninety-four. Her two grandsons both married American wives, and the younger, Charles, had an important political career. He was appointed secretary of the US Navy by Theodore Roosevelt in 1905, and a year and a half later, he became Attorney-General of the USA. He

had no children, and his nephew Jérôme Napoleon, who died in 1945, was the last American Bonaparte.

The 'bad Lucien branch' became notorious principally through Lucien's fourth son, Pierre. The second son died young, and the two elder sons were notable scholars, the elder as an ornithologist, the younger as a philologist. As a soldier of fortune, Pierre fought

The trial of Pierre Bonaparte
for the murder of Victor
Noir: a contemporary print.
Pierre was known as 'the
Corsican wild boar' on
account of the outrageous life
of adventure he led.

in the South American revolutions, in Albania and in Turkey.
After 1848 he was elected a deputy from Corsica, recognized as a
member of the imperial family and given an allowance of 100,000
francs a year. In January 1870 he shot a journalist, Victor Noir,
who called on him as a second, bearing a challenge to a duel.
Pierre was acquitted on the grounds of self-defence, but he

fled the country and the tottering Empire was discredited. His son, however, Prince Roland, married Marie Blanc, the heiress of the former waiter who created Monte-Carlo as a gambling resort, with a dowry of a million pounds. The only child of this marriage became Princess Marie of Greece, marrying the second son of the King of Greece.

Lucien's eldest daughter, Laetitia, also did not improve the reputation of the family. She married the son of an Irish baronet, Thomas Wyse, but left her husband, and had an illegitimate daughter, Studholmina, by a Captain Hodgson. She was not received at Napoleon III's Court, but had a pension. Her daughter Studholmina married Count Ferdinand de Solms, but her conduct became so flagrantly opposed to the regime that she was expelled from France, and lived at Aix in Savoy. She became the mistress of Rattazzi, the Italian politician, and later his wife, in 1863. Elisa's daughter Napoleone Camerata also lived in Paris on a pension. She dropped the name Camerata when she separated from her husband in 1830, and was known as Princess Bacciochi. The Beauharnais cousins were also looked after. A Count Tascher de la Pagerie was Grand Master of the Imperial Household, and his son First Chamberlain with salaries of 40,000 and 30,000 francs. All these allowances and pensions ceased with the fall of the Empire.

The first ten years of Napoléon III's reign had, at least in appearance, been brilliantly successful. In foreign policy he had succeeded in carrying out part of the programme of the Napoleonic Legend and *Les Idées Napoléoniennes*. France's participation in the Crimean War had completely altered the diplomatic scene. The Waterloo Coalition against France had been dissolved. France and Britain were fighting Russia as allies, and Austria was left in uneasy isolation. Queen Victoria was greatly impressed by Louis-Napoleon on his first state visit to London. She wrote to her uncle Leopold that:

He is evidently possessed of indomitable courage, unflinching firmness of purpose, self-reliance, perseverance and great secrecy; to this should be added a great reliance on what he calls his Star, and a belief in omens and incidents as connected with his future destiny, which is almost romantic – and at the same time he is endowed with wonderful self-control, great calmness, even gentleness, and with a power of fascination, the effect of which upon all those who become more intimately acquainted with him is most sensibly felt.

OPPOSITE Prince Roland, son of the wild Pierre, seated in his gallery.

OVERLEAF The Empress Eugénie out driving in the Champs-Elysées: a contemporary print.

S. M. L'Impératrice d

L'Escorte de l'Impératrice

Hortense Cornu, who had known him from childhood, said:

I have known him build castles in the air and live in them for years. . . . When he was young he had two fixed ideas – to be the Emperor of France and the liberator of Italy, and I do not believe that even now he has abandoned the latter. Like most men of imagination he lives in the future; as a child his desire was to become a historical character. His intellectual character has great excellence and great deficiencies. He has no originality or invention; he has no power of reasoning or rather of discussing; he has few fixed or general principles of any kind. But he is a very acute observer, particularly of the weaknesses and follies of those around him. There is as much discrepancy in his moral qualities. He is exceedingly mild and kind; his friendships are steady, though his passions are not. He has in a high degree decision, obstinacy, dissimulation, patience and self-reliance. He is not stopped or turned out of his course by any scruples. What we call a sum of right and wrong, he calls prejudice. His courage and determination are perfect, but he is exceedingly indolent and procrastinating, and his habitual suspicion deprives him of much assistance from others.

The Peace Congress of Paris of 1856 represents the high watermark of France's prestige under the Second Empire.

Italy as the next stage of the legend was never far from Louis-Napoleon's thoughts. Piedmontese troops had fought in the Crimea, though Cavour failed to obtain representation at the Congress as a reward. But the Italian question was briefly raised on the Agenda of the Conference at the end by Walewski and Clarendon. When Cavour left Paris, Louis-Napoleon told him, 'I have a presentiment that the present peace will not last long.'

Action was hastened by the Orsini bomb plot. In January 1858 bombs were thrown at the Emperor's carriage as he was attending the opera. The imperial couple escaped unhurt, but eight people were killed and 150 injured. Louis-Napoleon would have preferred to reprieve Orsini, had not public opinion been so outraged. But he turned the trial into a moving manifesto for Italian liberation, and allowed a letter from Orsini to be read which said, 'May your Majesty not reject the last prayer of a patriot on the steps of the scaffold. Let him liberate my country: and the blessings of its twenty-five million citizens will follow him through the ages.'

In July 1858 he met Cavour secretly at Plombières, and it was agreed that the aim of a war should be a Piedmontese kingdom of

Lombardy, Venetia, the Romagna and the duchies, a central Italian kingdom of Tuscany, the Papal States and Naples – all to form a Confederation under the presidency of the Pope. In return for two hundred thousand French troops, Piedmont was to cede Nice and Savoy to France.

In April 1859 Austria was goaded into becoming the aggressor by demanding the disarmament of Piedmont. Louis-Napoleon won the battles of Magenta and Solferino, and expelled the Austrians from Lombardy, but the armistice of Villafranca which followed was dictated by two considerations. The balance of numbers was now tipping against the French, and there were rumours that Prussia was mobilizing on the Rhine. Secondly, the nationalist movement in Central Italy was demanding annexation to Piedmont. In 1860, Napoleon had to watch helplessly while Garibaldi conquered the south for Piedmont, and the Pope was left in Rome dependent on the protection of a French garrison. Instead of a Federation under the Pope, Louis-Napoleon was faced with a unitary Italy, which was not grateful to France because France deprived her of Venetia and Rome. Cavour had outwitted Louis-Napoleon, and the nationality principle had turned out disturbingly different from the legend.

In the 1860s, Napoleon III had to deal with the infinitely more formidable Bismarck, and his health was already deteriorating. He was suffering agonies of pain and discomfort from the stone in the bladder which finally killed him. The Italian War had forfeited him the English alliance, because the annexation of Nice and Savoy aroused traditional English fears of an aggressive Bonapartist France, and there was an acute phase of naval rivalry. His intervention in the Polish revolt of 1863 lost him the entente with Russia. Involvement in the Mexican adventure tied up substantial French military forces overseas at a time when the German question was being stirred up by Bismarck.

In October 1864, Bismarck talked with Louis-Napoleon at Biarritz, and came away convinced that Napoleon would not intervene in a Prussian war with Austria. Louis-Napoleon was acting on the fatal assumption that an Austro-Prussian war would be either long or an Austrian victory. He told Walewski that, 'War between Austria and Prussia is one of those unhoped-for happenings that never seemed likely to occur; and it is not for us to oppose warlike intentions which contain so many advantages for our policy.'

A supper in the theatre of the Tuileries, during
an international exhibition of 1867: the painting is by Baron.

The Prussian victory of Sadowa was, however, recognized as a defeat for France, but Napoleon III overruled his Council and refused to allow armed intervention on the Rhine. Bismarck insisted on a quick armistice with Austria in order to switch troops to the Rhine to forestall French intervention. Napoleon III's subsequent proposals for 'compensation' on the Rhine were rebuffed by Bismarck. He similarly vetoed the proposal for a voluntary transfer of Luxembourg to France. Not much comfort was to be found in the independence of the south German States, and French public opinion was so desperate that the least provocation would cause an explosion. This came with the news of the Hohenzollern candidature for the throne of Spain in 1870. Bismarck no doubt viewed it as a diplomatic success for Prussia, but he preferred war in 1870 to a later date, before France's rearmament could get under way. The completion of the Liberal Empire in 1870

Caricatures of the Emperor and his wife from a series entitled *La Ménagerie Impériale*. Napoleon is depicted as a vulture and Eugénie as a crane, the characteristics of the first being cowardice and ferocity and those of the second, posturing and stupidity.

LA MÉNAGERIE IMPÉRIALE.

NAPOLÉON III

N° 1

LE VAUTOUR (Lâcheté-Férocité)

LA MÉNAGERIE IMPÉRIALE.

EUGÉNIE

N° 2

LA GRUE (Pose-Bêtise)

DÉPOSÉ — Tous droits reservés

DÉPOSÉ — Tous droits réservés

with the Ollivier ministry, and the subsequent plebiscite which gave seven million votes in favour, seem to show that the regime of the Empire was stronger than ever. But the governmental machinery was in disarray, and when the war crisis came, the responsibility for decision-making was uncertain. France won an unexpected diplomatic victory when the Hohenzollern candidate to Spain withdrew and then revised the position by demanding guarantees from the King of Prussia that it would not be renewed. This gave Bismarck the opportunity to edit the telegram so as to make war certain. It is clear that the Cabinet, pushed by bellicose public opinion, was responsible for these decisions rather than the Emperor and Empress.

Napoleon III's responsibility lay in his failure to restrain the Ministers through feebleness of will undermined by his health. He knew better than anyone the weak state of the French army,

HISTOIRE

DES

AMOURS, SCANDALES ET LIBERTINAGES

DES BONAPARTE

MARGUERITE BELLANGER (d'après une photographie de Disdéri,) ET SON DOUX SEIGNEUR

A cartoon showing Napoleon III with his favourite mistress, Marguerite Bellanger. She was rumoured (falsely) to be the daughter of a hangman and was the most universally loathed of Napoleon's mistresses.

207

and he was desperately trying to get into production the new breech-loading field-gun to match the Krupp guns. It was Ollivier who said that he entered the war 'with a light heart'.

When Napoleon III surrendered with his army at Sedan, the Prince Imperial, who was on campaign with his father, had been sent to Belgium. When the news of Sedan arrived in Paris, the dynasty was deposed, and Eugénie escaped to England with the help of her American dentist. She was reunited with the Prince Imperial, and rented a house, Camden Place, in Chislehurst, Kent. There was no lack of money, as Eugénie had sold some of her jewels for £150,000; Napoleon III had £60,000 in cash, and property in Italy. Napoleon III was interned for six months in Wilhelmshöhe, which had been Jérôme's palace when he was King of Westphalia. Here he was visited for two days by Eugénie, and in March he arrived at Camden Place. His resignation in exile, his refusal to blame anybody for the débâcle, were remarkable and admirable, and in marked contrast to his uncle's behaviour at St Helena. The exiles had not given up hope of a restoration. Napoleon III was, at sixty-three, physically worn out, but all his hopes were centred on his son, who in turn was devoted to his father. When a Bonapartist was elected to the National Assembly for Corsica early in 1872, hopes revived. A necessary part of any plan was to tackle Napoleon's health-problem. The doctors recommended an operation for crushing the large stone in his bladder, but he died suddenly after three operations.

Plon-Plon attended the funeral, confident that now, as head of the House of Bonaparte, he would have the guardianship of the Prince Imperial in his minority, and control of the Bonapartist party. He was frustrated by Napoleon's Will, which left everything to Eugénie. He accused Eugénie of destroying a later Will, and demanded guardianship of the Prince Imperial. The split was open, and Plon-Plon refused to attend the celebrations for the Prince's coming-of-age in March 1874. His speech aroused delirious enthusiasm among the Bonapartist faithful. He was turning out to be both an attractive and a sensible young man. As head of the Bonapartist party, he was in no hurry to act; he was completing his military studies at Woolwich, and realized that he had to prove himself as a soldier in the Bonaparte tradition. In appearance and many of his personal qualities, he had inherited more of the Montijo than of the Bonaparte strain. Queen Victoria was as fond of the Prince Imperial as she was of Eugénie, and there were

OPPOSITE The Prince Imperial in military uniform. He was poised on the brink of a successful military career, with the possibility of marriage to one of Queen Victoria's daughters, when he met his tragic death at the hands of the Zulus – a tribe whom he in fact admired.

rumours that she favoured a marriage between the Prince Imperial and the youngest daughter, Beatrice. She wrote that, 'For the peace of Europe the Queen thinks it would be best if the Prince Imperial was ultimately to succeed.'

It was owing to this friendship that the Prince Imperial was able to get his way and join the British army fighting the Zulu war in 1879. After the shocking defeat of Isandhlwana, it had become a full-scale war, and the Prince's battery was on its way to South Africa. His request to the Commander-in-Chief to be allowed to join it was turned down, but he was so upset by the refusal that he persuaded his mother, who in turn put pressure on Queen Victoria. The military authorities changed their mind, but it was made clear to the Prince Imperial that he was being allowed to go as a spectator only. Disraeli, as Prime Minister, said afterwards, 'My conscience is clear. I did all that I could to stop his going. But what can you do when you have two obstinate women to deal with?' Lord Chelmsford, the local commander-in-chief, was embarrassed and alarmed by the Prince's keenness and recklessness on reconnaissances. He assigned him a harmless task in drawing up plans for a fort, and he was sent out on a mission to select the next day's site for a camp. As the party led by Captain Cary rested, they were ambushed by Zulus. In mounting his horse, the Prince Imperial's holster strap broke, and he fell, left behind. Alone, he was speared to death by eighteen wounds from the Zulu assegais.

The negligence of Captain Cary was inexplicable. If he had turned round when he saw that the Prince Imperial was not following, his party would probably have frightened off the Zulus. The tragedy was not only an appalling shock to Eugénie but a severe embarrassment to the British army and government. There were ugly rumours and accusations in France that the Prince Imperial had been deliberately disposed of by the British. Captain Cary was court-martialled and it was only on the intervention of Eugénie that he was not cashiered. But he was ostracized by his brother-officers.

The premature and unnecessary death of the Prince Imperial ruined the prospects of the Bonapartist party. Plon-Plon was not an acceptable candidate, and the split continued. In his Will the Prince Imperial confided the fortunes of the Bonapartist party not to Plon-Plon but to his eldest son Prince Victor. 'When I am dead the task of continuing the work of Napoleon I and of Napoleon III will devolve upon the eldest son of Prince Napoleon.' There were now two factions, the Jérômists and Victoriens. Prince Victor, moreover, did not have the same appeal, the same conviction in his cause, as the Prince Imperial. In the 1880s the Third Republic ran into serious difficulties, and General Boulanger emerged as the 'strong man' who challenged the Republic; when the test came, he proved to be a broken reed. If the Prince Imperial had been available in these years, he would have been a far more attractive alternative to the Republic, and might well have succeeded in a restoration of the Empire.

In 1885 the Republic banished from France all heads of former reigning families and their direct heirs. Plon-Plon and both his sons left France. Plon-Plon died in 1891; Prince Victor took up

Prince Victor-Napoleon, who married into the Belgian royal family. His wife Clémentine proved, in the eyes of her friends, more Bonapartist than Victor himself, and she was well read in all the literature of the Bonapartes.

residence in Brussels, and his brother Louis became a General in the Russian army. In 1910, at the age of fifty, Victor married Princess Clémentine, youngest daughter of King Leopold II of the Belgians. It is his son, Prince Napoleon, born in 1914, who is the Bonaparte Pretender today, since the death of his father in 1926. He married Alix de Foresta, and has two sons and two daughters. He served in the Foreign Legion incognito, and in the Resistance in the Second World War, being awarded the Croix de Guerre and made Chevalier de la Légion d'Honneur. As the ban on the former dynasties of France has been lifted, he lives in Paris or at Prangins, which he inherited from his uncle Prince Louis.

In 1880 Eugénie insisted on visiting Natal to see the spot where her son was killed, and on her way back she stopped at St Helena. In 1881 she moved from Chislehurst to Farnborough Hill, and built a memorial chapel to hold the tomb of Napoleon III, the Prince Imperial and herself. She lived on, incredibly, to the age of ninety-five. She died in 1920, having lived to see the revenge for Sedan, the allied victory of 1918 and the Versailles Treaty. Now the tombs of all three are tended by the monks of St Michael's Abbey of Farnborough.

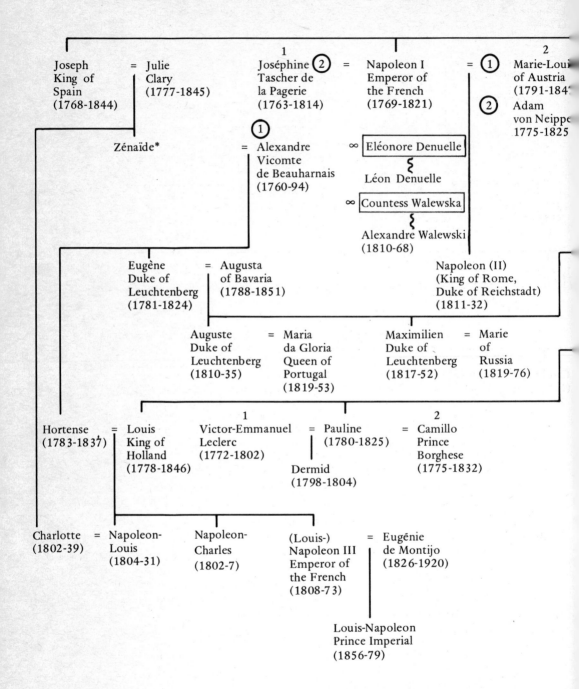

Joseph
King of
Spain
(1768-1844)

= Julie
Clary
(1777-1845)

1

Joséphine ②
Tascher de
la Pagerie
(1763-1814)

= Napoleon I
Emperor of
the French
(1769-1821)

= ①

2

Marie-Lou·
of Austria
(1791-184·

② Adam
von Neippe
1775-1825

Zénaïde*

①

= Alexandre
Vicomte
de Beauharnais
(1760-94)

∞ Eléonore Denuelle

Léon Denuelle

∞ Countess Walewska

Alexandre Walewski
(1810-68)

Eugène
Duke of
Leuchtenberg
(1781-1824)

= Augusta
of Bavaria
(1788-1851)

Napoleon (II)
(King of Rome,
Duke of Reichstadt)
(1811-32)

Auguste
Duke of
Leuchtenberg
(1810-35)

= Maria
da Gloria
Queen of
Portugal
(1819-53)

Maximilien
Duke of
Leuchtenberg
(1817-52)

= Marie
of
Russia
(1819-76)

1

Victor-Emmanuel
Leclerc
(1772-1802)

= Pauline
(1780-1825)

Dermid
(1798-1804)

2

= Camillo
Prince
Borghese
(1775-1832)

Hortense
(1783-1837)

= Louis
King of
Holland
(1778-1846)

Charlotte
(1802-39)

= Napoleon-
Louis
(1804-31)

Napoleon-
Charles
(1802-7)

(Louis-)
Napoleon III
Emperor of
the French
(1808-73)

= Eugénie
de Montijo
(1826-1920)

Louis-Napoleon
Prince Imperial
(1856-79)

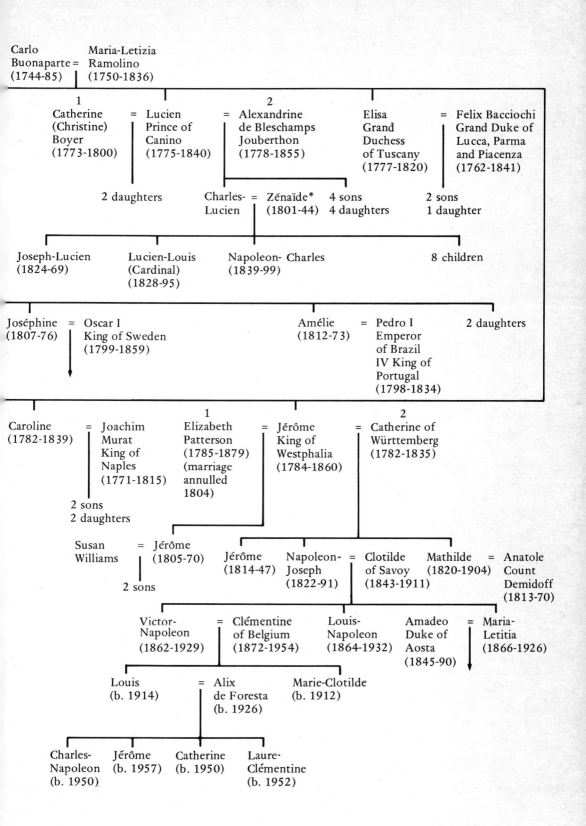

Carlo
Buonaparte = Maria-Letizia
(1744-85) | Ramolino
(1750-1836)

1
Catherine
(Christine) = Lucien
Boyer   Prince of
(1773-1800) Canino
             (1775-1840)

2
= Alexandrine
  de Bleschamps
  Joubourthon
  (1778-1855)

Elisa
Grand
Duchess
of Tuscany
(1777-1820)

= Felix Bacciochi
  Grand Duke of
  Lucca, Parma
  and Piacenza
  (1762-1841)

2 daughters

Charles- = Zénaïde*   4 sons
Lucien   (1801-44)   4 daughters

2 sons
1 daughter

Joseph-Lucien
(1824-69)

Lucien-Louis
(Cardinal)
(1828-95)

Napoleon- Charles
(1839-99)

8 children

Joséphine = Oscar I
(1807-76)   King of Sweden
            (1799-1859)

Amélie = Pedro I
(1812-73) Emperor
          of Brazil
          IV King of
          Portugal
          (1798-1834)

2 daughters

Caroline = Joachim
(1782-1839) Murat
            King of
            Naples
            (1771-1815)

1
Elizabeth
Patterson = Jérôme
(1785-1879) King of
(marriage   Westphalia
annulled   (1784-1860)
1804)

2
= Catherine of
  Württemberg
  (1782-1835)

2 sons
2 daughters

Susan = Jérôme
Williams (1805-70)

Jérôme
(1814-47)

Napoleon- = Clotilde
Joseph   of Savoy
(1822-91)   (1843-1911)

Mathilde = Anatole
(1820-1904) Count
            Demidoff
            (1813-70)

2 sons

Victor- = Clémentine
Napoleon of Belgium
(1862-1929) (1872-1954)

Louis-
Napoleon
(1864-1932)

Amadeo
Duke of
Aosta
(1845-90)

= Maria-
  Letitia
  (1866-1926)

Louis = Alix
(b. 1914) de Foresta
          (b. 1926)

Marie-Clotilde
(b. 1912)

Charles-
Napoleon
(b. 1950)

Jérôme
(b. 1957)

Catherine
(b. 1950)

Laure-
Clémentine
(b. 1952)

Acknowledgments

The author and publisher would like to thank the following museums, institutions and photographers for supplying the illustrations reproduced on the pages listed below:

A. C. Cooper Ltd 38–9; Agence France-Presse 213; Archives Nationales, Paris 19, 51, 112; Bibliothèque de la Ville de Paris 36; Bibliothèque du Musée de l'Armée 115–5; Bibliothèque Nationale, Paris, endpaper, 9, 15 (Jean-Pierre Vieil), 16–17, 32–3, 62, 69, 142–3, 154–5, 183, 207; Bulloz, Paris 9, 10–11, 18–19, 20, 25, 30, 32–3, 46–7, 51, 58–9, 66, 67, 77, 78, 88–9, 90–1, 92, 99, 100 (private collection), 104, 108, 114–15, 118–19, 124, 142–3, 146, 150–1, 153, 154–5, 161, 162 (bottom), 166 (Collection du Prince Murat), 187, 200–1, 204–5; Jean-Loup Charmet 52, 97, 136, 158–9, 176–7; Collection Bonnat à Bayonne 92; Collection du Comte de Penha-Longa 49; René Dazy 41; John Freeman 132–3, 139; Giraudon, Paris 2, 12, 29, 34, 39, 49, 54, 62, 70, 71, 73, 74–5, 82–3, 106–7, 120, 123, 144, 165, 170–1, 179, 190, 191; Mansell Collection 94–5; Musée de l'Ile de France, Sceaux 54; Musée de la Legion d'Honneur 88–9; Musée de Toulon 165; Musée du Louvre, Paris 30, 82–3, 84, 99; Musée Marmottan 170–1; Musée Napoleon à Arenenberg 66; Musée National du Château de Compiègne 191, 204–5; Musée National du Château de Malmaison 28, 39, 120, 144; Musée National du Château de Versailles 12, 46–7, 58–9, 73, 74–5, 77, 78, 90–1, 104, 106–7, 108, 118–19, 124, 161, 187, 190, 206 (left and right); Radio Times Hulton Picture Library 162 (top), 192, 195, 208, 211; Réunion des Musées Nationaux 84; Royal Palace, Stockholm 34; Savitz Learning Resource Centre, Glassboro State College, New Jersey 167; Staatliche Kunstsammlungen, Cassel 123; Jean-Pierre Vieil 96; H. Roger Viollet, endpaper, 36, 69, 111, 112, 128–9, 149, 169, 183, 196–7, 198, 207, 212; Westminster Libraries, London 38–9.

Picture research by Ann Mitchell.

Bibliography

Aronson, T., *The Golden Bees* (Oldbourne 1964).

Bear, J., *Caroline Murat* (Collins 1972).

Bartel, P., *La Jeunesse Inédite de Napoléon* (Amiot-Dumont 1954).

Castelot, A., *L'Aiglon, Napoléon Deux* (Le Livre Contemporain 1959).

Cole, H., *The Betrayers, Joachim and Caroline Murat* (Eyre Methuen 1972).

Connelly, O., *The Gentle Bonaparte* (Macmillan, New York 1968). (ed. Webb, V.) *Napoleon's Satellite Kingdoms* (Free Press, US 1971).

Decaux, A., *Letitia, Mère de l'Empereur* (Fayard 1959).

Delderfield, R. F., *The Golden Millstones* (Weidenfeld and Nicolson 1964).

Dixon, Pierson, *Pauline* (Collins 1964).

Geer, W., *Napoleon and his Family* (Brentano's, New York 1927–9).

Holt, E., *Plon-Plon, the Life of Prince Napoleon* (Michael Joseph 1973).

Knapton, E., *Empress Josephine* (Oxford University Press 1964 and Penguin 1969).

Kurtz, H., *The Empress Eugénie* (Hamish Hamilton 1964).

Marceggi, J., *La Genèse de Napoleon* (Perrin 1902).

Markham, F., *Napoleon* (Weidenfeld and Nicolson 1963).

Masson, F., *Napoléon et sa Famille* (Ollendorff 1900–1919).

Oman, C., *Napoleon's Viceroy, Eugène de Beauharnais* (Hodder and Stoughton 1966).

Richardson, J., *Princesse Mathilde* (Weidenfeld and Nicolson 1969).

Stacton, D., *The Bonapartes* (Hodder and Stoughton 1966).

Stirling, M., *A Pride of Lions* (Collins 1961).

Thompson, J. M., *Louis Napoleon* (Blackwell 1954).

Weiner, M., *The Parvenu Princesses: Elisa, Pauline and Caroline Bonaparte* (John Murray 1967).

Bonaparte-Wyse, O., *The Spurious Brood: Princess Letizia and her Children* (Gollancz 1969).

Index